IT'S AN ODD THING, BUT . . .

BY THE SAME AUTHOR

Oddly Enough
Even Oddlier
Oddly Bodlikins
Next to Oddliness
Model Oddlies
Gladly Oddly
Idly Oddly
I Said Oddly, Diddle I?
Oodles of Oddlies
Oddly Ad Lib
I Was Joking, Of Course

PAUL JENNINGS

It's An Odd Thing, But . . .

MAX REINHARDT
LONDON SYDNEY
TORONTO

¢ Acknowledgements

These pieces have appeared in *Punch*, the *Telegraph Magazine*, the *Observer*, the *Guardian*, the *Tablet*, the *Sunday Times* and the *Ford Times*. Some more than others, of course, but things keep changing all the time. The last piece, *The Pseudo-Pitman*, appears here for the first time.

ISBN 0 370 01457 X
Printed and bound in Great Britain for
Max Reinhardt Ltd
9 Bow Street, London WC2 E7AL
by C. Tinling & Co. Ltd, Prescot
Set in Linotype Plantin
First published 1971

¢ Contents

UNPOP WORDS

¢ Let the People Choose, that's Popular, isn't it?

'BUT THAT'S enough about the future, and our plans to make this little island of ours the world's greatest producer and exporter of pop, a leader in the Third Industrial Revolution, the Revolution of Leisure. I know what you are all waiting for. Ladies and gentlemen, the first Natmuspol Top Twenty!'

An expectant hush fell on the gathering of well-known pop stars, civil servants, elderly beatniks from the posh mass media, and photographers. Lord Nemo pulled aside the curtain which covered most of one wall and revealed a large screen of some kind of frosted glass. He pressed a switch and the following list appeared, in letters of brilliant white light.

1. Norman C. Webb (The Singing Dentist). (*Er were floyin' arf, hur, hur.*)
2. The Meritocracy. (*Hands Up, the Anal Erotics.*)
3. The Five Census. (*Deedle Eedle Ee.*)
4. The Hairy Fairies. (*Ah Doan Tew No.*)
5. Penelope Longanimity. (*My Heart is a Lonely Flower.*)
6. The Egg Breakers. (*Don't Change Sex, Baby.*)
7. Otto Klemperer and his Hot 82. (*Big Ludwig.*)
8. The Doomsday Men. (*Ma Baby got Green Hair.*)
9. Count John McCormack. (Re-issue, *Irish Airs* from *Dhonnh Gheoibannhi,* by *Mho Tsaeiouart.*)
10. Annie Flesh. (*Ah wannabee wan.*)

11. The Unquiet Gravediggers. (*Trees.*)
12. The Hypodermics. (*Vamp Till Ready, Then Add Batter.*)
13. Hamilton Academicals. (*Tam O'Rating.*)
14. Rock de Vere. (*Man, You Can't Have My Baby.*)
15. Phil Harm and the Moany Us. (*Runcorn Rock.*)
16. Brixton Road Liberal Skiffle Group. (*The Proportional Representation Song.*)
17. The Lord Goodman Trio. (*Nackety Yabber.*)
18. The Bodkins. (*Mindless Rage Rock.*)
19. The Creakers. (*I Love You, Teilhard de Chardin.*)
20. The LSD. (*That Old Chinese Junk.*)

Since the occasion was being televised those of the second to twentieth place-holders who were present erupted into hearty show-biz applause as Norman C. Webb stepped up to receive from the hands of Lord Nemo the very first 'Max' (as the monthly Maximum Sales Award had instantly been dubbed by the press; it was a hideous EPNS figure of Narcissus). Even the Acne of Perfection, a group who had been around so long that they seemed a permanent part of the pop landscape, joined in, although this was the first time for three years they had been unplaced.

Lord Nemo's speech was, as usual, a political masterpiece. He rejoiced not only that the first winner should have been a dentist, a member of the so-called 'professional' classes, thus destroying the old shibboleth of a relationship between class and culture—this was simply the *people*'s art of the future—but also that he was a *rural* dentist. He was a link with our great popular tradition of folk-song. He himself did not pretend to know all the words of Mr Webb's delightful song (laughter). But he could guess what it was about (loud laughter). Seriously, though, love was an international theme, and he hoped that, indeed he could *see* by their generous applause that groups such as The Egg Breakers or The Bodkins, who had carried Britain's fame to the remotest corners of the earth, would not begrudge Mr Webb his success, nor would Mr Webb be unmindful that their great work in, as it were, popularizing pop had helped create the conditions in which he could revitalize our old heritage of song. Unless a people sang it would die. And so on.

Nemo had been the obvious choice as first director of Natmuspol or, to give it its full title, the National Music Poll. A tone-deaf lawyer, he was the kind of politician who, in his youth, has decided to be a politician long before he decides what party to belong to, so that his political coloration seems a kind of accident; it is somehow bad form to say out loud to such a one, if he is a Conservative, that it is odd for him to support some mammoth redevelopment stunt in which house-owners are subject to compulsory purchase and eviction, or, if he is a Socialist, that it is odd for him to send his children to exclusive public schools; it is as bad form to do this as twenty years ago it was to accuse someone of having a religion. Lord Nemo just knew in his bones, and had influentially said so at many secret dinner-tables, that pop music (together with football the chief enthusiasm of the post-war average man) was an immense social force, the control of which was essential to the government—*any* government. 'If it can Beat, man, join it,' he would say to his intimates with a wintry smile.

It was largely on his advice that Natmuspol had been founded, the official reason being that existing methods of establishing the Top Twenty were haphazard and unreliable. Instead of rival and conflicting claims by private-enterprise pop music papers, the BBC and record companies, there would be this one official monthly list, impartial, scientific, compiled by a Government-organized computer service linked operationally with the research facilities of the Central Office of Information. It was a rationalization which would also help pop music to its rightful place among our exports —above marmalade, hand-made shoes, Kendal mint cake, whisky, Jaguars; perhaps earning even more dollars than the tourist trade. There were, at first, a few faint protests under the slogan 'Rationalization is Nationalization', but in general the pop industry welcomed Natmuspol both because it removed much of the financial hit-or-miss element and because Nemo had cunningly embodied a tax-rebate scheme.

For the first few days the authorities were gratified by what seemed the extraordinary accuracy of Natmuspol's computer, the Public Reaction Enumerator, Songs of Light Entertainment (Youth), usually referred to by its initials as PRESLEY. By the end of ten days Norman C. Webb's disc had sold the unprecedented number of 17 million. It was clear that many people were buying more than one copy.

It soon became disturbingly clear why. *Nobody bought anything else*. Whether because PRESLEY actually *was* scientifically accurate, as contrasted with the hidden promotion efforts in the old Top Twenty lists, or because Natmuspol publicity had simply convinced everyone that it was, people were now simply not interested in anything but the authentic, one and only top record. The whole system of buying something because a lot of other people bought it (fast developing in other arts, notably the book world, divided into best-sellers and no-sellers), instead of by personal taste and be damned to what everyone else is buying, now reached its logical conclusion. To all, from the chance buyer to those who regularly bought one or more discs every week, it seemed a waste of money to buy anything but the best. And the best was no longer something involving doubt and troublesome personal decision; there it was, undeniable, objectively and impartially determined, *Er were floyin' arf, hur, hur,* by Norman C. Webb, the Singing Dentist.

In vain The Hermaphrodites brought out *My Dolly's a Mixture,* Annie Flesh *I Long to Belong* and the Doomsday Men *When A Chinaman Yells He's A Feller Yeller, Not A Yeller Feller* (a peace song). In vain some groups tried the regional idiom of Norman C. Webb; the Hairy Fairies' pressing of *Oi Were a Floyboy, Martal Zure* sold not one single copy. Progress and change seemed stopped in their tracks. By the end of the month Norman C. Webb's sales had zoomed to 33½ million. He was a nice simple man, an honest amateur who had only sung at dentists' conferences until the day when his brother-in-law, an ambitious man who had now abandoned accountancy to become his manager, persuaded him to make a tape, and he was as embarrassed as anyone by the whole thing.

The original Natmuspol plan had been for a monthly Announcement Party, similar to the opening one. But as the day for the second list drew near, checks on the computer made it inexorably clear that there wasn't going to be a Top Twenty. Just a Top One. The needle had stuck, with a vengeance. The party was cancelled, while Nemo and his board held urgent meetings to decide what to do next. After all, they could not just repudiate PRESLEY. It had functioned perfectly correctly; it had not been used to persuade, merely to collate and record, although on a scale hitherto unapproached. No one had foreseen how compellingly its authority would eliminate minority tastes in an area where sales and value were interchangeable terms.

In the event matters were taken out of their hands. In the confusion the cancellation notices were not sent out, and even as the board were deliberating there was an increasing hubbub from the great reception hall below; the enraged Nos. 2 to 20, and many more besides, were breaking up the place and smashing up PRESLEY with fire-axes (in the old free-for-all system, which subsequently came back into operation, an unknown group from Nuneaton called the Luddites leapt into the third place with *Break It Up*).

'Oughtn't we to phone for the police, Lord Nemo?' said a pale-faced board member, as the shouting, crashing and splintering sounds from below rose in a *crescendo*.

'No, no,' said Nemo, 'let them be. Pop isn't all *that* important. But elections are, so far. This thing has given me an idea.'

¢ Business Notes

> '... the big majority of the finance for musical performances comes from the audiences and those private business interests that employ musicians'—PEP Report on The Sponsorship of Music.

A sharp, buffeting wind, of the special city kind that comes suddenly round the corners of high buildings, whirling scraps of paper and dust, seeming colder than it really is after the warmth of restaurant doorways and the human contact of crowds, flattened Gilbert Prothero's thin overcoat against his body. His gaunt, slightly stooping figure, the aquiline face with deep-set liquid brown eyes, the long straight silver hair under the wide hat, might have made him a conspicuous figure in the quiet Edgbaston road where he had lived for some thirty years, but here in Soho he passed unnoticed.

'I'm like one of the old buildings; some of us haven't changed,' he thought ironically to himself. And indeed he had an obvious affinity with that curious inner decent and domestic heart of Soho, where in contrast to the bulging fleshiness of strip clubs, quilted and studded satin seats, forgettable faces in which carelessly poured flesh seems to have obscured the bones, the people have something taut, vertical, inward and withdrawn about them, matched by the secret and uncommunicative blocks, guarded by old green or maroon railings, where their families may be glimpsed through lace curtains having serious meals, with soup, or mothers may be heard calling to their children in Italian.

It was to just such a block that Prothero now made his way; although a jazzy front office had been put into the Orpheus Agency, most of the interior was still stone steps, brown linoleum corridors and little offices with gas fires.

At first he thought he had mistaken the address and that the girl was sitting under a hair-drier of a curiously dead pink-lemon colour. But then he saw that the monstrous tea-cosy was in fact the actual hair of the receptionist. He approached the desk diffidently.

'Are you pop, Pop?' she asked.

'No, unpop, I'm afraid,' sighed Prothero. 'I wonder if—'

She flipped through a card-index. 'Well, we only got a two-day down at Torquay. Bongo, double on vibes. You'll have—'

'I have an appointment with Mr Scharpenwitz.'

'Ah, that's different. Whyncha say so? What name?'

Prothero told her. The incredulity with which she looked at him over the telephone changed to surprised respect. 'He says to go up straight away, Mr Profumo. Take the lift. You can't miss it, he's got the whole first floor, wall-to-wall and everything.'

Monty Scharpenwitz greeted his visitor warmly. 'Gil, you don't changed a bit since we sat at the second desk under Landon Ronald. Haven't seen you since I left for the old Armstrong-Vickers Philharmonic. I was only playing there two, three years, they had a new manager, he only liked Strauss, Waldteufel—such schmaltz! So it was the Armstrong-Vickers Light Concert Orchestra. Or was it Vickers-Armstrong? Vickers-schmickers, I should remember, so long ago! All that 'm-ta-ta, 'm-ta-ta, 'm-ta-ta, I left and started this agency. I done all right, Gil. Looka this.' He opened an enormous drink cupboard. 'What you want? Armagnac, champagne, Campari, seven kinds of sherry, five kinds of gin. You gotta impress these tycoons. I had Sir Halford Reddish in here the other day.'

'Who's he?'

'Gil, where you been all this time? Rugby Portland Cement Symphony, they just been on a world tour, Boulez conducted them in Paris, he said he never heard woodwind like it. That's why Sir Halford came, he wants someone can play the *ondes martenot*. I got a lovely boy can do the musical saw, I told him no one would know the difference, but he wouldn't have it, wanted the proper thing. Still, that's my problem. What's with you? You been with the CBSO, all that time?'

'I've been in Birmingham, Monty, but not with the CBSO. Newman Briggs & Crowther Quartet.'

'Of course, I remember. The best. I still got your record of that Haydn, what is it? The Lark? The Dream? The Sunrise? The Frog? Funny they all got names.'

'We recorded them all, while old Mr Newman was alive. He was the old school, you know. I don't think he cared for anything after Brahms.'

'I had this idea he was German.'

'Oh yes. He was Ulrich Neumann, he came over before the first war. He got this connection with Crowther's Flange & Grommet Company, then not much more than a workshop down in Digbeth. Old Crowther had died when I joined them, but he was a real old Birmingham craftsman, with genius in his hands, who came up the hard way; he put his boy through Cambridge—he's export manager now, a very good amateur viola player, I used to let him play with us now and again when Lajos was off ill or after some woman.'

'Ach, these Hungarians! It's the Tokay!'

'But a good chap—and what a tone! The Hollywood

and the Amadeus did their damnedest to get him, you know, but he stayed with us to the end. Well, as I was saying, old Neumann teamed up with Crowther and with Briggs as secretary the thing went ahead like wildfire, we moved out to a great new place in Saltley, in 1927 I think it was. We must have worked through the entire Haydn-Mozart-Beethoven repertoire several times. Divertimenti before the weekly Director's dinner, very often one of the late Beethovens after; old Newman said his idea of heaven was Opus 135 with a light brandy. Then there was the work-people's Tuesday concert; it started half an hour before knocking-off time, and I can tell you that NBC's claim to have the most musical workers in Birmingham was no idle boast.'

'So what for you leaving them now?'

'There's been a take-over. Old Newman would never have allowed it. But the son was never interested really, and he's sold out to Universal Brass. It all comes under their Personnel Department in London now, a frightful woman called Miss Carfax; she only wants us to stay at all if we work as professional stiffening in a works band —and UB have just brought in a three-shift system that makes rehearsal impossible, as she well knows.'

'Gil, I wish I could help you. But chamber guys, even top ones like you, they're a drug on the market. People want the big sound now. Second tymp. I could give you with ICI. BMC are yelling for a principal clarinet. Hey, wait, there *is* the Dunlop Bach Choir; they do the B Minor every year, they want a leader. That's in your area somewhere, isn't it—Castle Bromwich, West Bromwich, Bromyard, Bromley, Fort Sunshine, something like that. But you'd probably have to lend a hand with chorus training.'

'Monty, I'm too old to change. I've got some sort of a pension, and I daresay I can stick it out.'

'For you, I can offer leader with Rolls-Royce. They do a lot of Walton, Honegger, stuff like that. Pro rata for concertos. And you might have to bone up on Milhaud and like that if the Concorde gets off the ground.'

'It's kind of you Monty, but no thanks. Chamber or nothing.'

Prothero got up to go. Then he hesitated. 'Have you got that "Lark" record here?' he asked.

Scharpenwitz flipped expertly along the shelf of records and picked out the box. He opened the console of an enormous but elegant hi-fi. In silence the two listened to the perfect, gay and formal music, given an added, far-off astringency by the thin 78 recording. There was silence when it ended. Then Scharpenwitz said simply, 'You're quite right, Gil. That's what it's all about. Hold on to it, boy. And if I don't write you in six weeks' time to tell you I've sold a quartet to Unilever, my name ain't Monty Scharpenwitz.'

¢ Never Mind about the Sense, it's a Wonderful Sound

✦✦

BE HONEST; how far down do you have to read the following lines (from which the first three words have been omitted because they would give the game away) before you twig?

. . . dhie änn-dsch'l didd seh,
Uoz tuh sört'n puhr schep-pörds inn fihlds äs dheh leh
In fihlds äs dheh leh kiehping dhär schiep
Onn eh kohld uinters naitt dhätt uos so dihp.

You've got it? Good. Here, for comparison, is the French version:

. . . dze enne-dj'l dide sé,
Huozz tou seurt'n pou'eur chepp-eurdes inne fildes aze dzé lé,
Inne fildes aze dzé lé kipinng dzère chipe
Onne é caulde ouinn-t'r's naïte dzatte houozz sau dipe

You *have* got it. The missing words are *dhie först Noel*, or if you prefer it, *dze feurste Noel.* And I haven't just made them up either; they are all the recommended phonetic pronunciations in the Hugo German and French dictionaries.

Nobody is going to tell me after this that one can get too subjective or imaginative (and they did, on one paper) about the sound of words. Those phonetic words were made up on a strictly objective and practical basis, as a quick approximation to the sounds of their own language, to help foreigners pronounce English; there was absolutely no attempt at onomatopoeia or beauty or association. But who will deny the exquisite appropriateness of *änn-dsch'l* for a German angel—so much better even than their own word *Engel*? An *änn-dsch'l* makes exactly that crisp rustling sound with his wings, partly the sound of tinsel in a warm interior and partly the sound of wind through northern conifers on a metallically *kohld uinters naitt*.

The French, on the other hand, is much closer to the Mediterranean or Near East where, after all, Christmas began. There is a hint almost of the *djinn* about an *enne-dj'l*—a mysterious winged presence, felt rather than seen, in the clear desert night. Maybe the French colonial experience in North Africa has something to do with *ouinn-t'r* (obviously a dried-up oasis) and *houozz* (an unoccupied fort with caches of food, water, etc., for use by infrequent patrols and expeditions). But I doubt it.

Perhaps, not surprisingly, this note is even better sustained in a carol specifically referring to the East:

Oui tsrie kinngs ove auriennte âre
Bèr-inng guiftes oui trav-eurse afare
File annde fâ-ounn-tinne, mou'r annde mâ-ounn-tinne
Foll-au-ing i'onn-d'r starre;
O, starre ove ou-onn-d'r, starre ove nâite
Starre ouidz roa-i-al bioue-ti brâite
Ouesstouarde lîd-inng, stille pro-cîdinng
Lide osse tou dzâi peur-ficte lâite.

It seems to me that the third line of this gives us a much clearer, and at the same time more poetic and beautiful picture of the landscape through which the Magi travelled, than the stock Victorian 'field and fountain, moor and mountain'. These are very localizing, if not actually incongruous words, setting the scene in

Scotland or Yorkshire. Whatever the Magi crossed, it was not moors. They went through a landscape of hard and symbolic rocks, even though, as Eliot says, later

Then at dawn we came down to a temperate valley,
Wet, below the snow line, smelling of vegetation;
With a running stream and a water-mill beating
the darkness

but not across moors. They rode wearily but purposefully past terrifying lunar escarpments, *mâ-ounn-tinne,* and dreadful abysses, *fâ-ounn-tinne,* in which boomed mocking empty voices, and picked their way along many a *mou'r,* dried-up river bed. And if there are not old legends in which the Star, to the Arabian astronomers who spoke the sonorous names of Betelgeuse and Aldebaran, is known as *I'onn-d'r,* I shall be very surprised.

Or let us consider the Spanish:

Gud king Wenceslas lukd aut
On de fiist ov Steven
Juen de snou lei raund abaut
Diip and krisp and ii-vn;
Braitli shonn de muun dat nait
Dou de froast uoas kruu-el
Juen ei pur man keim in sait
Gadaring uinta fiuel.

This takes us right back from the conventional baroque and Castilian Spain to something much older and more basic, with no rot about accents; the Spain of the guttural Pyrenean languages, Basque, Catalan, with all those uncompromising short words and those k's. We are back in the legendary *Song of Roland* times, we perceive misty heroes like Braitli and Gadaring, their bright swords flashing in far-off battles against the Moors under Ii-vn. The carol has the primitive strength and haunting simplicity of those very early Spanish wooden statues.

It isn't exactly an international language (after all one has to consider the phonetic words given the other way round, when an English member of a German carol party, for instance, would be singing *Hile-igge nahkt*); all the same it is pleasant to think of foreigners among us uniting in song, perhaps even starting or ending the performance with

Godde sève âour grécheuse Couine
Lonng live âour nauble Couine
Godde sève âour Couine.
Sennde her victaurieuse
Hăppi and glaurieuse
Lonng tou règn auv'r össe
Godde sève âour Couine.

. . . or, as the case may be

Godd sehw aur grehschoss Kuiehn
Longg liw aur nohbl Kuiehn
Godd sehw aur Kuiehn
Sennd her wiktorious
Häpi annd gloarioss
Longg tuh rehn ohwr ass
Godd sehw aur Kuiehn

. . . a very different matter. But in fact carol parties are usually less formal than this, being for the most part in the open air. One can imagine a quartet, quite good musically, meeting for one rehearsal of all the old favourites at the home of the English organizer, William (tenor). The others are Genevieve (soprano), a rather serious girl with glasses and long hair, from Lyons, doing a post-graduate year in London; Hans (bass), a young German engineer who has married an English girl (but she doesn't sing) and settled here; and Maria, the Spanish au-pair girl, a slightly raspy contralto.

'Let's start with *Ding Dong Merrily on High,*' says William, handing out the music.

'Huott is *Dingg Dongg Merili Onn Hei*?' says Hans. 'Kudd uie nott stahrt uidh *Heilige Nacht*? Itt is eh werri bjuhtiful Dschörmann karol, huitsch ewribodi nohs.'

'Ladies first, Hans,' says William equably. 'It's French so Genevieve will know it.'

'Inne France oui doue notte sinng itte inne dzisse oué,' says Genevieve. Nevertheless they have a shot at it, but Maria gets lost in all those runs in the Gloria. 'It is raada ei komplikeited figuereishun,' she says, with her indolent smile at William. She is rather keen on him.

On the second try they manage quite well but something goes wrong with the intonation, they end slightly flat.

'Ai tsinnque peur-hâpes dze baisse ize é litteul flatte,' says Genevieve (correctly, as it happens, but tactlessly).

'Juh ahr misstehk'n,' replies Hans. 'Ai häw pörr-fekt pitsch.' But they stick to it, William being a good diplomat as well as musician; and in the end their voices, blending marvellously as they sing in a harmony given added sonority on a still and frosty night when it echoes against the high walls of a London square, cause one door after another to be opened; and more than one entranced hearer tells them: 'I have never heard the words so beautifully before.'

¢ When it's Rāgtime in King's Road

'Annigoni's pupil Timothy Whidborne ... lent his King's Road studio for a party for his friend Julie Felix to celebrate her new record *Saturday Night* ... Michael Caine, Simon Dee, Mike Sarne and playwright John Mortimer were among the ones who turned up before the drink ran out. Paul McCartney and David Frost were too late ... Donovan, who wrote the song for Julie, didn't turn up at all. "Miss Felix was rather upset about that," said her manager. "Donovan hates parties, but he was supposed to come to this one." Donovan, it appears, was having sitar lessons from George Harrison at the time.'—*Daily Mail.*

Scene: Another part of the forest.
Hari Sonh: What dost thou seek?
Dhana Vanh: Master, I seek a new sound.
Hari Sonh: To the ear of Brahma all sounds are the same sound.
Dhana Vanh: It may be so, for those who have trod the path of perfection.
Hari Sonh: Wouldst thou tread such a path? It is a path not shown on any chart.
Dhana Vanh: How then didst thou attain it, Master, if thou followedst not the charts?
Hari Sonh: The charts followed me. To Brahma it is the same thing.
Dhana Vanh: What then must I do?
Hari Sonh: First thou must sweep out my hut for one year.

Dhana Vanh: Master, I see no hut. Thy abode is rich, even as the people told me on my journey hither.
Hari Sonh: Aimez-vous Brahma?
Dhana Vanh: The people told me thou wast witty too.
Hari Sonh: The new sound thou seekest is truly an old sound.
Dhana Vanh: I have sought thee because the people are weary of the old sound.
Hari Sonh: Thou must distinguish between the old sound, which I, even I will teach thee, and the recent sound, which is as the rolling of stones, the straightening of kinks, or the cry of animals.
Dhana Vanh: Or the droning of beetles.
Hari Sonh: Thou must sweep out my hut for *two* years.
Dhana Vanh: Were there not three others with thee when thou troddedst—
Hari Sonh: Trodst.
Dhana Vanh: Were there not three others with thee when thou didst tread the road of perfection?
Hari Sonh: Thou must sweep out my hut for *three* years.
Dhana Vanh: Swepst—
Hari Sonh: Lasteth the whole drink through.
Dhana Vanh: Ahaha. Diddest thou sweep out thy guru's hut for three years before thou learnedst thy skill on the sitar?
Hari Sonh: Thou mustest not ask me that kind of question. *I* am the guru, not the other way round.
Dhana Vanh: What, thou meanest like *urug*?
Hari Sonh: *Urug*? What gibberish gibberest thou?
Dhana Vanh: *Guru* the other way round, like thou saidest. *Urug*. Hey, listen, I got an idea for a song. *Urug, Urug, ma lerve is lahk a drug*. The kids'll love it,

everybody'll say '*Urug*, what's it mean?' It'll be the in-word. *Urug, urug.*

Hari Sonh: Good day to thee. I see thou art not ready for the Way of Enlightenment.

Dhana Vanh: Nay, Master, wax not wroth.

Hari Sonh: I never wax, wack.

Dhana Vanh: Thou art lucky. I must make many more waxings before I get a hut like this.

Hari Sonh: Thou art young, therefore will I help thee and be thy guru.

Dhana Vanh: I knewest thou would help me. Couldst I then have a lesson on the sitar, without sweeping out thy hut?

Hari Sonh: It is usual to sweep out the hut. Why art thou in such a hurry?

Dhana Vanh: I am bidden to a fesst in the Road of the King.

Hari Sonh: Thou foolish boy, thou wilst never get anywhere if thou goest to feasts when thou shouldst be practising the sitar. It is not easy, thou knowest. It is not an electronic sitar; although there are often sympathetic strings, thou hast to make all the noise thyself.

Dhana Vanh: In truth I hate feasts, Master. But I am supposed to go to this one.

Hari Sonh: Why?

Dhana Vanh: Everybody will be there.

Hari Sonh: *I* shall not be there, wack.

Dhana Vanh: Michael Caine, David Frost, John Mortimer ... everybody, nobody. What the hell! To Brahma it is all the same thing.

Hari Sonh: I see thou art learning. Well, now, come into my humble hut. Take this sitar and sit down on that charpoy with it.

Dhana Vanh: Oh, is it a bed-sitar?

Hari Sonh: One more crack, wack, and thou art out on thy ear.
Dhana Vanh: Upon what principles doth the old music (which to Brahma is even as the new) rest?
Hari Sonh: First, thou must rid thy ear of Western harmony.
Dhana Vanh: That will be easy.
Hari Sonh: Then thou must learn that in classical Indian music the player improvises on a *rāga,* or *rāg.* A *rāga,* or *rāg,* is a series of notes within the octave, differentiated from any other *rāga* by the prominence of certain fixed notes and by the sequence of particular notes.
Dhana Vanh: Analogous to a tone-row, in fact?
Hari Sonh: Who told thee that? Yes, like a tone-row. To the ear of Brahma it is all the same. Now, there are *rāgas* for different emotions, and even for different times of day. The question of the systematic classification of the *rāgas* presents considerable difficulty. For the past 350 years the south has had a more or less uniform system; northern musicians, however, have had as many systems as musicians. Sarngadeva enumerates 264 *rāgas* under the two *grāmas.* The *Rāga Vibodha* adopts the southern system and recognizes twenty-three primary *rāgas* with a large number of secondary *rāgas.* The primary *rāgas* of this work are *Mukhārī* (i.e. Kanakāngi), Revagupta, Sāmavarālī, Todī, Nādarāmakriyā, Bhairava, Vasanta, Vasanta-Bhairava, Mālavagaula, Ritigaula, Abhīranāta—
Dhana Vanh: Which one of these is Tiger Rāg?
Hari Sonh: Get thee gone to thy feast. And next time bring a broom.

ℭ Just Keep Your Teeth out of the Theatre

SURELY IT is time to call a halt to the spate of plays about lechery among dentists?

First there was *The Complaisant Lover,* by Graham Greene, about a dentist's *ménage à trois*; and then there was *Cactus Flower* (adapted, as I'm sure you all know, by Abe Burrows from Pierre Barillet and Jean Pierre Grédy), in which Margaret Leighton played one of those did-anyone-ever-tell-you-you-are-beautiful-without-those-glasses parts as receptionist to someone who sounds very unlike all the dentists *I* have ever known, with their aura of white light and silence against which is etched a formalized routine of tiny whirring and clinking sounds and monosyllables murmured to obedient quiet girls like secular nuns in rooms of Japanese dignity and austerity.

One pillar of society after another has fallen, more and more absolutes have become relative, what with marrying monsignori, the replacement of steam by diesel, the Bishop of Woolwich's God, the pound sterling, and even divorced persons in the Royal Enclosure. But *dentists*! No wonder two such plays seem like a spate; something ultimate has been challenged, some last citadel of certainty stormed.

It's a mistake to think that doctors are grander than dentists just because they know about stuff below the neck as well. (By that analogy vets are grander than doctors, since after all doctors only have to know about the human body, but a vet is supposed to know about everything from a cow to a mouse—and cows have seven stomachs to begin with; a doctor may be able to tell you what is wrong with your lungs, but the vet has to know whether a snake *has* lungs.) Perhaps because of their concern with the whole human person, often spilling over into mental or emotional realms, doctors remain personal, fallible figures. They have made a bold, almost cavalier assault on an infinite subject, accepting that there are still wide areas of ignorance or error.

But dentists, spurning the excitement and glory of this, have chosen to restrict their equally good minds to something by now almost perfect. Surely no major improvement is now possible to those superbly functional, gently hissing chairs, those tiny meticulous X-rays? Dentists not only prevent big pain with injections, they (mine, at any rate) prevent, unasked, the negligible pain of the injection itself with some kind of magic pad. Their drills become ever more supersonic and instantaneous, their instruments ever more classically perfect; they know, and can perform, everything to do with teeth. Their world is beautiful, ordered, rational (yet tough, involving blood and a certain physical strength). No dentist has bad breath.

Who, reading his old school's magazine, has not noted that Prince, J.T., or Adams, F. is taking his finals in dentistry at Belfast, or Birmingham, or London, and not remembered some sober, kind, decent, quiet, generous boy and thought, Ah yes, I can just see *him* as a dentist? The term 'medical student' instantly conjures up drinking, bawdy songs, spirited rags before that word became debased; but the mind simply has no picture of a dental students' rag. Even those who will later become owlish economists and work for Unilever now have guitar-ins at the LSE, but I have never read of such doings in those imagined solemn buildings, set in their own grounds, in residential roads in Belfast or Birmingham. I bet if dental students had a rag it would be called a cloth, at least.

Doctors are used to cheerful nicknames like *sawbones, head-shrinker, quack, medico*; and it would be very easy to invent similar jokey terms for dentists, such as *gumsmith, jawbones, fangwright, ivory dealer, mouth organizer, yank manager*. But no one bothers to invent them because everyone knows they would not stick. A dentist is a dentist is a dentist.

This isn't only true of British dentists. True, I did once have a Czech dentist who regaled me with extraordinary stories of his brother, an inventor in trouble with the police because his anti-car-thief device, which shot a two-inch bolt from under the driver's seat, had very nearly killed a man ('but he *was* a thief,' said my dentist indignantly); and in the Queen's University Medical Library of that very same Belfast one may read, in *Diseases of the Paradentium,* by Dr Martin Akopian, translated from the Armenian by H. Ovanessian, how the author's experiment ploughed through the sterile theories of 'the Localists, the Fusionists, and, most important, the Constitutionalists'; how, after he had operated in Moscow on 'a forty-five-year-old fat general' with pyorrhoea, the rival professor who had sent the patient, seeing the inflamed tissues the next day, said, 'Look here, fellow, we spent a whole month in order to calm the patient's irritated and inflamed gingiva. What a rubbish you have done.' Not surprisingly, the Constitutionalists formed committees to look into his case. '. . . some threatened "jokingly" to kill me. My wife was very much alarmed and worried. She feared that the doctors might poison me and that our children might be orphaned. She often shed tears. I laughed at her simplicity.' (She was right, though, because he was eventually exiled to 'a place in the eskimos' country'.)

But both these cases merely confirm what one had assumed, that dentists can have very strong views, like anyone else. They do not offer the slightest basis for this threatened new wave of Dentistry Drama. God knows the medical profession has been ill enough served by what might be called the Theatre of Operations, with stuff like *Dr Kildare* and *Dr Finlay's Casebook* and *Emergency—Ward 10*. But it is accepted by all as light, escapist, *television* stuff (not for me, I'd rather talk about my own operations than view other people's). It would be a different matter with a real genuine live theatre movement.

Once it became the smart thing, Dentistry Drama would affect real life as other fashions in the live theatre have. Look how smart Pinter has made the inability to communicate. Look at the angry young man image countless adolescents have grown up into since Osborne invented the first one. Mark my words, if dramatists (an opportunist lot who know a good thing when they see it, and will recognize instinctively that lust among dentists has more box-office potential than a harem in a sacristy) do not exercise self-restraint, the last bastion will go.

No longer shall we wait in neat rooms where, first thing every morning, the piles of colour supplements (or, in the older ones, of *Punch*) have been tidied. We shall sink uneasily, in the sick half-light behind undrawn curtains, on to a rumpled divan, the only furniture in the room. A pouting slattern in a tight sweater will come in and start half-heartedly collecting empty gin bottles and glasses. There will be a heavy tread on the stairs, the door will burst open and the dentist will lurch in.

'Goddam, Maggie,' he will say to the girl, 'how'd I know she'd come back yest'day, now the alimony's fixed. I——' then seeing us, 'O h'llo, mister. You're the wisdom bicuspid, aren't you? Gee, I got the shakes today. Well, come on in here. You too, Maggie, I want lots an' lots of amaglam. Amalgalam. Amalagam. Well, you know. Like I showed you yest'day. In that little dish. Siddown in that chair, mister. Like a cinema organ, eh? *Up,* down, *up,* down. *Wheee*! Right, open your mouth, less have a look . . .'

I'm warning them. We can give up going to the theatre, but not going to the dentist.

MOVING WORDS

¢ Trouble at t'Airport

(A memory of the BOAC pilots' strike)

✦✦

IN THE grim little airline towns within an hour or so's drive from Heathrow (Sunningdale, Ascot, Woking, Leatherhead, Kingston, Maidenhead)—places whose dour, closely-knit people have been identified with the flying industry since the bad old balloon-and-stringbag days—there is an eerie silence instead of the roar of jets. In happier days the fierce folk loyalty of these people would be expressed in the famous gatherings at White Waltham or Farnborough; no one who has heard the crowds of pilots and their wives and often quite tiny children, after the long open-air day of processions, carnival fun and ripcord dancing displays, as they bawl out the lusty old favourities like *Don't Go Up In the Plane Daddy,* can ever forget the extraordinary sense of unity forged in the sweat of a hard, traditional craft; a craft which, as is too often forgotten, was one of the foundations of Britain's modern greatness.

But today the outsider is aware of hostile glances, especially if he is from the press, which these sturdy pilot-folk all regard as being on the side of the boss class and the hated Guthrie. Sullen groups of pilots, the fag-ends of Corona Coronas or other duty-free cheap cigars dangling from their lower lips, stand aimlessly at street corners or dawdle endlessly, in Skindles' or the Castle Hotel, Windsor, over champagne cocktails and the ubiquitous home counties delicacy, 'smoked salmon'.

In the simple detached residences, often without

colour television and standing in less than an acre of gardens, they are preparing for a long siege.

I spoke to Mrs Venetia Sopwith-Vere-Benson, a grim-faced pilot's wife whom I met outside one such typical home, as she struggled to unload a case of a dozen Beaujolais from her car, a Mini with well over 5,000 miles on the clock.

'This is all we can manage for a second car. If some of them at Whitehall were to come down here and see for themselves what it's like trying to live on a captain's wages of £5,800 a year they wouldn't talk so fancy about us holding the nation to ransom, and the balance of payments. What about *our* balance of payments? Let them try scrimping and scraping to pay for the filtration plant on a miserable thirty-foot swimming pool!'

This is a town with long, bitter memories going back to the 'George' Strike, when the pilots came out against the controversial automatic pilot—one of the many issues still plaguing the industry after the inconclusive settlement of 1948. 'Aye,' said Mrs Sopwith-Vere-Benson, 'there's many here recall the George Strike. That's why I've got this stuff. Several wine merchants refused credit altogether. We had a hell of a job to keep the Sunday morning patio parties going at all; but they're an institution in these parts, and somehow we managed with beer and stuff. But this time BALPA are going to help us with the banks, and we're getting this stuff from the Duty-free. Most of us wives are with the Drivers and the Men Up Front to hell or harry prangers. But why am I saying all this to the filthy, revisionist, Guthrie-toadying, BALPA-hating press, where it's always harry clampers on the truth and justice of our claims?'

But the minds of these sorely-tried workers are not

entirely closed, and after a few hundred-pound notes had changed hands her husband, Toby Sopwith-Vere-Benson, a sky-steward and district convener of BALPA, agreed to smuggle me into their meeting to discuss the Guthrie offer of an extra £75 a week.

'It's derisory, old boy, they'll turn it down harry nem-conners. Guthrie really wants to break BALPA this time. The so-called settlement of the George Strike broke the old unwieldy GAU (General Airline Union); harry shambles, old boy, and now the industry's full of breakaway unions like NUTS (Navigators Union and Trade Society) and RATS (Radio and Allied Types Staff), riddled with Trots and scabs and Guthrie spies. In the old days GAU spoke for the old unit of the trade, the Cot (crew of three, old boy). Captain, Engineer and Steward. Each could pretty well do the other's job in the old Imperial Airways days. There was comradeship, variety. Often I'd pour out the tea for the passenger bods in their wicker chairs, the steward would get out on the wing to tighten up some loose wire and the engineer would bring the old kite down harry plonkers on the grass at Hendon.

'It was a tough life, and many people scraped and saved to get their boys into nice comfortable jobs like stockbroking or property speculation—anything but up in the dreaded air like their fathers. But at least we were together. After the George Strike we were too disunited to cope with either nationalization or the awful boredom of the pilot's job, all those little dials to watch, and not even a private toilet for him. But really BALPA is fighting for everyone. You'll see, old boy.'

I sensed the passion and purpose of these men the moment my eyes became accustomed to the dim lighting of the austere, red-plush ballroom of the simple four-star hotel where their secret meetings are held. They began with a full-throated rendering of the BALPA Revolutionary Hymn:

Onward, brothers of the skies
Though management wildly rages
Confound those dastards, shame their lies
And fight for honest wages
From old Heathrow to Idlewild
Our glorious banner streaming
Fly, comrades, honour undefiled
To salaries past dreaming
We who guide the mighty jet
Through stormy skies and sunny
As the planes grow mightier yet
Want lots and lots more money
Bold captains on our worldwide rounds
Let no boss try to reason
On! On! To thirteen thousand pounds!
One penny less is treason.

As my guide had predicted, the £75 offer was rejected with howls of execration, and as I slipped out unobtrusively they were excitedly discussing plans for a sleep-in at the BOAC terminal at Victoria and the burning of Sir Giles Guthrie in effigy. It will be a tough fight, and one can only hope that out of the despair of Sunningdale, Ascot, Woking, Leatherhead and the rest, out of the old tragedy and heartbreak of this violent and passionate industry, a new hope will eventually be born.

¢ The Proletairiat

✦✦

A STRANGE THING about air travel is that it gets less romantic and *other* as the aircraft get more sophisticated. This hasn't happened with cars. However boring the man you see in a Rolls-Royce may actually be, there is always a lingering possibility that when his chauffeur gets him out of this traffic jam of the common people he will go home to a discreet and impenetrable mansion full of joy and light, where some quality flows from his Picassos and Renoirs into *him* (after all, even Berenson was rich before he became Mr Renaissance, not the other way round).

Maybe he can buy not only culture but even innocence, on some island where, under the heavy tinkling of fronds in a warm breeze, he observes sunny lawns stretching away to mountains, and bright birds flash through the air exorcising all guilt with their song. Maybe his wife greets him with a grave smile, no words being needed, in a kitchen with the decent splendour of a sacristy, where she is doing something basically, unattainably simple—boiling an egg, perhaps, with the help of the gold egg-timer containing a reddish powder (crushed rubies?) which I saw in a shop in Regent Street the other day.

Early air travellers had some of this otherness. Firbankian figures in teddy-bear coats got into great shuddering machines with many engines and four-bladed screws which special men (*Morning, Sir George, Morning, Harry*) had to pull to start them, afterwards leaping back on to the grass, their wide trousers flapping in a primitive gale as they waved goodbye. Those passengers sat in cabins like tiny green Palm Courts, with wicker chairs. Some were called Mitzi, Bunny, Hohenlohe, Mdivani. In flying boats they came down, the feathery wake a brilliant event in some warm sea far from the Depression.

Then there was an intermediate stage, when all aeroplanes had retractable undercarriages but still preferred to go round the Alps, carrying people at least as *other* as export managers, which of course is not very. But now immense jets packed with suave electronic devices sail nonchalantly over Mont Blanc, flying saloon bars containing 120 people with more ordinary and less other faces than one sees on a train to, say, Ipswich. They seem to lack purpose, the journey is not an occasion for them. It is as though they had got on to the wrong escalator at Gloucester Road or somewhere and had suddenly found themselves off to Turin or Istanbul, and when they arrive there they will blink vaguely in the bright sunshine, apathetically have a coffee, get into another jet and come back.

Hundreds of thousands more of these people will be required by the new generation of supersonic airliners, doing the 3,000 miles from London to New York in an hour with 300 passengers. Aircraft are only economic while they are in the air; so allowing an hour for each refuelling this means that every aircraft will have to do 12 journeys each day, six each way. That's 1,800 people per aircraft entering a country each day. Let us assume the modest figure of 10 airlines with four each of these aircraft (and it's bound to be more); that's 72,000 people a day—mostly, by this time, brigands, failed dictators, the groundsmen of very small parks, bootlace-tip salesmen, bankrupt stationers, ex-tramdrivers, and insurance clerks with vague intentions of becoming professional yodellers.

The airport will be choked, special hutted camps will have to be set up, overcrowded breeding grounds for passport and ticket forgery and other crime, for disaffection and epidemics. Harassed, underpaid staff will sit at trestle tables trying to sort out confusing claims to reservations and nationality from shouting queues, through which export managers and others with purpose in their journey will have to fight a perilous way.

Moreover, because of the genetic effects of radiation at supersonic flight heights on young women of reproductive age, the rabble on these aircraft will have to be controlled by *elderly hostesses* (this has been officially stated by better authorities than me). It won't be much use one of *them* beginning a long story 'I remember once dear Mr Balfour saying to my father . . .' to a mob of illiterate uprooted peasants munching and chomping highly seasoned food from old canvas bags and grunting to one another in some brutal patois, dicing, quarrelling over women. Something much more in the policewoman, even the wardress line will be called for.

But there is hope. Paradoxically the very speed of the new aircraft may lead to a rebirth of the old otherness. A 3,000-m.p.h. plane leaving New York at 9 a.m. will arrive after its one-hour journey, at 3 p.m., but going the other way, that is leaving London at 9 a.m., it will get to New York at 5 a.m., taking minus four hours. This will add another to the many ways in which the rich can buy youth; even four hours is not to be despised, and as the planes get ever quicker this will, of course, be increased. The rich will come by boat from New York, slowly enough for this time effect not to be noticeable at all; and they will fly back, getting younger every time, at fares high enough to make it economic for eastbound boats and westbound aircraft to carry the rabble, who will, of course, age correspondingly. There will be immense space and luxury for their small parties of blue-rinse ladies, men in teddy-bear coats, elderly hostesses, getting younger and gayer all the time. I'm not quite sure which way the export managers will go.

ℂ Feeble Torque

I WAS AT a party the other night where there was one of these chaps who really do know all about cars and whose current vehicle is some mysterious thing he made himself from a kit, which always surprises me (I mean you'd think once they'd made all the bits it would be cheaper to stick them together in the factory while they're at it, instead of packing them all separately and printing complicated instruction books and the rest of it). You'd expect anything made like that, however expert the assembler with his vast garage and his neat array of tools and his know-how, to come out looking faintly home-made; but not a bit of it, it's one of those terrific hard ochre-looking fastbacks about three-foot-six high, with a fascia like part of a Boeing cockpit and two or three gears still in hand when it's already doing 70 mph after 8 seconds or something (so what's the point of it in England—but let's not go into that now).

Anyway, during one of those unfortunate lulls in the conversation this chap was heard saying: 'Of course, with that ratio your torque converter is a problem.' (At least that's what I think he said.) At this, one of those girls with a piercing upper-class voice who are always telling you about 'the little man' who came to fix the washing-up machine said, with that amusing wave of the hand from the wrist only : 'Eeoo, I always thought a talk converter was one of those instant translation machines they have at the United Nations.'

Well, of course, everybody laughed—but I wasn't quite sure where I stood in all this. Well, yes, I am sure really. I come slap bang in the middle, between those who think it makes them seem intellectual and artistic to say airily they haven't the faintest idea what goes on under the bonnet and those who write to motoring magazines those incredibly (to me) knowledgeable letters.

'The No. 2 exhaust valve on my 1965 Anglia has burnt out three times in 46,000 miles. With just one valve affected in this way, could it be that the compensating jet holder, a bronze insert in the PSE1-6 carb which is loose, is causing this bother . . .' J.R.C. Yorks.

Come off it, J.R.C., that's not a letter, it's an essay—and if you know that much why didn't you tighten up that bronze insert before writing?

Now, I know what an exhaust valve is. I know all that basic stuff about the four strokes (Intake, Compression, Firing, Exhaust; new readers begin HERE); but it's no good asking me exactly what a venturi (or come to that a torque converter) is, and I have no idea whether *my* carb is a PSE1-6. And when it comes to things like the Wankel engine, I *have* tried, but the only way I can visualize it working is for the engine to keep still while the whole car turns over and over on it—and that can't be right.

Yet, I once, with the not inconsiderable help of my brother-in-law (who, it so happens, is a final inspector at the end of the Ferguson tractor assembly line) took to pieces and reassembled an entire engine, doing all that stuff about Top Dead Centre and the timing chain, which I'm bound to admit is getting a bit hazy in my mind now.

The point is that the car on which I (all right then, we) did this didn't have a torque converter. Dammit, it only just had electric lights! It was a 1928 Austin 7, which I bought in 1938 for £8 (7/6 a week, as a matter of fact). When I came back from the Army in 1946 it had lain at the bottom of the garden in Coventry in the open for seven years. Bombs had gone off near it, the hood had rotted, the windscreen was an opaque yellow, there was a nest of fieldmice in the back. But its aluminium body was perfectly sound. We put four new plugs in, dried the magneto in the oven, shoved some petrol in, and she started second turn.

Ah (mumble mumble, dribble, chew on toothless gums), you don't call cars "she" now, but you did then.

After we did all this work on the Austin, famous in song and story, I went to Switzerland. I clambered all over the Alps in it, I was hit by a French lorry in it, I wrote articles about it for which the least remunerated brought me more than I had paid for it. But the thing is, I did understand how it worked. I understood magneto ignition. I understood the magneto's cunning little Vernier adjustment, a disc with 19 teeth on one side and 20 on the other. I understood the petrol feed system (very simple, gravity; the tank was higher than the engine and the stuff just *fell* down according to the well-known laws of I. Newton, none of this fiddle-faddle with pumps). The brakes all worked with cables (none of this bleeding-the-master-cylinder stuff).

But it's not a bit of good pretending I understand all the mysterious objects, many of them shaped like some kind of discus, which are packed under the modern bonnet (or hood, as we shall all eventually be pressured into calling it—and then what are we going to call the hood, eh? Maybe that's why, one by one, they're all stopping making convertibles. Can't think what to call the roof). I don't really understand coil ignition (what's that condenser for?), voltage regulators, overdrive, fuel injection and all those mysterious little sealed-off boxes and glands.

What's more, I don't think the makers *want* us to understand them. You look at the section called *Self-help on the Road* on p. 7 of the AA Handbook. At first sight this is a masterly, logical analysis of the procedure if your car breaks down, beginning with *starter will not turn engine* (but what about *starter itself won't start,* or *starter makes despondent growling noise*?).

Many of the recommended actions I simply wouldn't dare. For *broken fan blade* it says *break off the opposite blade* (what, with your bare hands?). Above all, in a mere five pages, the recommended action in no less than 28 cases is: *consult agent.*

You see? You get this terrifying *sudden mechanical noise.* As it happens, it's 1.37 a.m. and you're on the A835, somewhere between Lubfearn and Lochdrum (don't ask me why. You were to have been guest of honour at a Masonic dinner in Lairg, still 26 miles away, but you had to break the opposite fan blade off back near North Berwick, or you dropped some carburettor bits into the engine outside Auchterhellweet. You were a spy helping the Chinese build a tunnel from Peking to Strathpeffer. You had a demon lover in the mountains. You were on your way to a sales conference in Dingwall and didn't realize it was so far. You couldn't sleep. *I* don't know. There are cars everywhere at all times now).

The map tells you the water on your right is Loch Glascarnoch, the dark high shape towering ominously on your left is Beinn Liath Mhor a' Ghuibhais Li. It is a wild night in February, with sleet threatening to turn to snow. You look in the AA book, and yes, there it is:

sudden mechanical noise. Stop immediately. Consult agent before moving on.

By the greatest good fortune there is a telephone box about a mile away along the shore of Loch Glascarnoch. Your agent lives in Beckenham, Kent, and 20 very complicated minutes later his phone rings and a musical Highland voice says, 'Wull ye be accepting a revairse-charge call from a Beinn Liath Mhor a' Ghuibhais Li call-box.' . . . But let us draw a veil over the rest of it.

Even the chaps who build their cars from kits aren't expected to be able to cope with any big trouble—they too have to do this agent-consulting lark.

Nonetheless, anything is better than seeming to belong to the my-dear-I-haven't-the-faintest-idea brigade—so what to do?

I don't think it helps very much if you simply lard your motoring conversation with bits of slang. If you talk about the *gear-stick* ('on the floor, proper place for it'), if you toss around phrases like 'one of my shockers is going' or 'I threw the anchors out' or even just *twin-carb,* unless you actually do wear a woolly cap and can assembly those kits you'll find yourself in deep water. Somebody will ask *you* about torque converters, and it won't help even if you have already looked this up in the encyclopaedia; in mine it says a lot of stuff about torque amplifiers, for steering great liners ('the operator applies a feeble torque to a control shaft that causes friction bands to engage with two drums rotating in opposite directions. The bands also engage with a shaft connected to the mechanism to be rotated . . . hence the feeble torque applied by the operator controls the extent to which the bands are brought into contact with the drum and . . .' ah, the hell with it. What do they mean, *hence*? And then suddenly there's a little paragraph at the end: 'the *torque converter* acts as an infinitely variable gear, usually with varying efficiency').

Short of going to night school you're never going to catch up with all this. Specific knowledge, the kind you have when you can connect a lot of meaningless paragraphs like that with this damned 'hence', is out. You are therefore left with two alternatives.

(1) You can dress up obvious general truths and make them sound like specific ones. Obviously manufacturers iron out bugs (what a curious expression, I've always thought; surely people never used this cumbrous method of getting rid of bugs, even before aerosols were invented?). It's easy to find out when the first of some popular series came out. Suppose, for instance, it was 1967—then you can say, 'I won't touch one pre-1969. They had terrible teething troubles with the steering/transmission/front-end/rear-end/suspension.'

(2) You can assume that *everyone,* including you, knows all about suspension, understeer, torque conversion and the rest of it, and talk of cars as architecture or art.

'The new ones have a hard-edge look.'

'I'm all for a baroque fascia myself.'

'Only the Japanese have this *instinct* for placing ashtrays.'

'What could be a more 19th-century concept, after all, than a glove-box?'

Secretly I cherish a hope that one day there will be (3)—kits for assembling neat little cars with aluminium bodies, magneto ignition, batteries under the seat and gravity petrol feed. Then *I* shall wear a woolly cap and come into my own.

ℭ Deus ex Machina (Rover, Of Course)

✦✦✦

WHENEVER POLISH car, which pretty seldom, article once read about Australia comes into mind. Writer was impressed by the way Australians are so practical, manly; they can all swim five miles, fix a half-shaft, castrate a bull-calf (what, in Sydney? I've seen pictures, a hilly street with buses and a lot of big square banks, looks just like any other city). Not like English, said article, who just *wash car* every weekend.

What so unmanly about washing car? Nobody *got* any bull-calves in our road. Can't leave mud on car on purpose, just to be manly. Would be like Bop Hope in that film about The West, he finds himself in den of frightful ruffians drinking out of huge glasses, saunters casually up to bar and says *give me a lemonade. In a dirty glass*. Have picture of manly man in muddy car, on way to mountains to do something manly, sneering out of window at people he sees washing cars.

All same, have obscure, probably quite justified feeling that am more manly than men who wash cars *every* weekend. *Weekend washer,* sounds even less manly than *weekend driver*. (And what wrong with weekend driver? Can't all be commercial travellers.) Wash mine when it colour of rhinoceros hide and bank balance even smaller than usual, or rather bigger than usual in red. Not because can't afford to have it done in garage (although, as matter of fact, can't. What can afford is relative, subjective matter; however rich was, having car washed, polished in garage would always seem unpardonable luxury, like paying man to shave you when you not ill or anything)—but because this when periodical thoughts of trade-in value recur. Must keep it in condition, perhaps rust eating fatally away already. Help, help, get polish, soft cloths etc., get back to unimaginable, lost-for-ever state when actually had money to buy, or start buying, this car new (how hell did it?).

Even while doing it know it pointless; if ever *do* trade in, won't make slightest difference whether take car as now, covered in mud, bare metal floor in back littered with gravel, plasticine, dolls' heads, cornflakes, tomatoes, old blood etc., or highly polished, with new carpets, four new tyres. Man will simply thumb through dog-eared list till he come to year and model and (by then) say '65 quid, take it or leave it, mister'.

Have to do job in road, Sunday morning. *Been* to church but feel faintly guilty (wasting water?) and foolish (unmanly?), stream of water running down road (it all very well for garage men, they have special slab of concrete with drain in middle). Also, at mercy of wife, children, at other end of hose on kitchen tap, invisible round corner. She accidentally, they on purpose turn up pressure, have to bawl TURN IT DOWN just when churchwarden-looking people passing.

Ha, rusty bit here. Get Touch-up Kit. Tiny tube of blue, mad intense concentrate, the way saccharine is, compared to sugar; have to mix it with white to get exact shade, called *Pompadour Blue* (doesn't sound so manly as *Monza Red*, must admit). Why Touch-up Kit not be simply one tube ready-mixed *Pompadour Blue*? Damn, made it too white. Add more blue. Damn, too blue. Quick, get it right, stuff drying on saucer already. It probably special cellulose paint, have to spray it at correct temperature etc., not fiddle about with bit on saucer. Damn, stepped backward, knocked over little pot of white. Bet Australians never knock paint over. But more *room* in Australia.

Own garage closed Sunday, drive to distant garage to get more Touch-up Kit. On way all drivers except me two types: Madman or Zombie. No, *three* types—Madman, Zombie and Rover. Something very special, *elected,* about people in Rovers, much more than Rolls-Royces. Rover can do 110 or something, a sight more than I can, but have never been passed by a Rover (and am not Madman, think). All Rovers go at 43 m.p.h. yet are quite different from Zombies. Zombies don't *know* when car behind them, they don't even know where they are going, they just sit behind lorry and hope dully it going somewhere nice. Behind bus they never anticipate it going to stop; when it stop, they do. But Rovermen know you there all right, see you in elegant solid mirror, courteously leave gap for you to pass. Rovermen have gear shift on floor, don't trust fancy gimmicks on steering column, they like it tight and solid, like everything else in Rover; lot of shiny wood.

Distant garage got no Pompadour Blue either, man stares when I ask for it. Very well, I say, like Bob Hope, give me some Wet and Dry (seem to remember that black abrasive paper called this). Yes, sir, says man, No. 1 or No. 3? Roverman buying eight gallons (always have three self; will fill tank when win Premium Bond, aha ha). Roverman says kindly, You'll probably want both; did I hear you ask for Pompadour Blue, *I have some in boot.*

He had, too. Beat that, Australia.

¢ They Shall not Pass

PSYCHIATRISTS HAVE known for some time about *viamnesia,* the mild detchment from reality that accompanies any form of motion and is today, of course, experienced chiefly by motorists. Men perfectly normal otherwise have strange semi-delusions, especially after a long run. Hills or giant cooling towers, that were on the right, or the left, suddenly disappear. They feel that their necks are made of lead or become convinced that thousands have mysteriously, suddenly died in the empty town they are passing through, and are standing or sitting in the attitudes of Pompeii behind those drawn curtains.

Viamnesia is not serious as long as the sufferer recognizes the symptoms and can treat himself, like a diabetic (chiefly by stopping and taking a few deep breaths). And although it has, strangely, only recently been discovered, the specialized form suffered by drivers of Wide Loads, *heviamnesia,* is also, fortunately, not incurable.

But it *is* strange that it hasn't been noticed before. A lady wrote to me years ago saying that *for four years running* every first week in May she had seen, at exactly the same point in Hampshire, a lorry with three men in paroxysms of laughter at great sacks of sugar spilt all over the road. I myself am absolutely certain that, driving from London, I saw just entering Stratford-on-Avon a huge lorry with a light railway engine (steam) and the next day saw this same load *leaving* Stratford. What had they been doing? Trying to sell it from door to door? Gone to the wrong Stratford? Found Clopton

Bridge collapsed into the Avon? Until recently, too, I was fairly sure of the existence of a thing called the A.J.O. (Anti-Jennings Organization) with head offices in Brentwood, that had bought eight old lightships, located on transporters at regional centres, which could be called up by radio whenever I was passing through.

I am relieved to hear that this isn't true, that it is, in fact, the *same* lightship with a driver suffering from heviamnesia, so that he simply wanders round the country with it. It is curious that psychiatrists never suspected before that 'normal' viamnesia, suffered in quite a small car, might be intensified when a man is driving something with 32 wheels carrying the east wing of a refinery or a steel ball 40 ft. high.

Yet the first authenticated case was only last year, when a director of Brobding, Nagg and Co., happening to follow an enormous transporter carrying one of his firm's gasometers down the North Circular Road one morning, noted the serial number and found himself behind it *going the other way* in the evening. Finding that this load had actually been dispatched three months previously he checked with other makers of gasometers, radio-telescopes, viaducts and giant boilers. One after another they found that while purchasers had assumed clerical errors in premature delivery notes, and manufacturers in non-acknowledgment, the drivers had been going all over the country.

Heviamnesia symptoms take various forms. Some drivers with vague memories of 'exports', drive from one port to another. Others simply go up and down the same stretch of road (*particularly* the North Circular). After the mounting tension, caused by the nagging suspicion that one of the 32 wheels has a puncture (but which?) the fear of meeting another Wide Load coming the other way, of stalling on a hill and finding that a block of flats has been caught on a projecting part of the load for the last three miles, any small untoward incident can bring on an attack, such as knocking over a clock tower or finding that one of the 137 bridges on the route is six inches too low.

Before this official explanation of heviamnesia every motorist will have had his own disturbing theories about experiences similar to that of the lady in Hampshire, or another one of mine only a month ago, when I saw a very large tanker going aimlessly among potato fields in Essex with a small sign at the back saying simply METHYLENE CHLORIDE. DANGEROUS VAPOUR. EMERGENCY TELEPHONE RUNCORN 2067.

I imagine this tanker bursting. The phone rings in a shed at Runcorn, on the sea side of the bridge across the Manchester Ship Canal. A placid elderly man in a vaguely nautical uniform removes his pipe, then frowns as the urgent words come tumbling over a bad line. 'Half a minute, let me write it down,' he says. 'Now M,E,T,H,Y,L—no, we haven't had a ship by that name through. Eh? Oh. Oh, ah, *oh.* You want Runcorn two o six *seven.* But they're all gone home now, I daresay . . .' Meanwhile, in some Essex village, in an emergency dispensary opened in the village hall, an overworked G.P. rattles the cradle furiously, shouting *Operator, operator!* while all round him potato farmers are lying down screeching with laughter, or turning blue, or shrinking, or whatever it is methylene chloride makes you do.

But now I can see with relief that the recent announcement in Parliament that the number of Wide Loads was being reduced was true after all. They are sending out a reduced number, an unavoidable minimum, of swing bridges, liner propellers and gasometers every week; with trained police psychiatrist escorts. But of course we shan't feel the effect of the reduction until all the lost heviamnesiacs have been tracked down.

¶ Meet Me under the Unmanned Halt Clock

AMBIVALENCE IS the thing nowadays. There's a lot of it about, even in the Catholic Church or British nationality. And another body to have lost the air it had, in one's youth, of pristine, we-were-here-first, unquestionable solidity, is British Rail, as the L.M.S., G.W.R. and L.N.E.R. are now laughingly called.

At Newmarket there is an example so extreme that one is forced to imagine the drama behind the scenes. For Newmarket (which is well known even in Japan, for one is always seeing photographs of Japanese buyers at bloodstock sales there) has a railway, still, but the station for this considerable place is a mere Unmanned Halt, and has been since 1967. But this change was made almost immediately after £40,000 *(forty thousand pounds) had been spent on modernizing the station, waiting rooms and ticket apparatus.*

The only possible explanation for this is ambivalence at the highest, decision-making level. The way I see it is this. The man behind the modernizing of the station was the leader of the expansionist party in Eastern Region, Col. d'Arcy-Poumphrey. He gravitated naturally to Newmarket in the course of his work for Special Station Unit, a project of portable stations for events that bring a sudden, once-only influx to small places with inadequate stations; a Boot Fair in Northampton, an International Shuttle Festival in some small Lancashire weaving town, any Eisteddfod.

The Colonel came late to British Railways, after a long period in the R.E.'s attached to the Indian Army, and a short spell on civilian accident enquiry work. In his hound's-tooth check suit, always sporting a brown bowler and with a carnation in his lapel, he soon acquired a reputation as 'the best-dressed man in British Railways', somewhat to the disgust of old B.R. men who had served their time with the old Chatham and Dover, the pink-liveried Basingstoke and West Hants, or the Metropolitan and Penge (with its unique Dragon-class peat-and-charcoal-burning 0-3-0 saddle-tank duplexes). But they had to admit that the Colonel knew his railways; Special Station Unit (SSU) was a success from the start.

However, he always had the dream of building a great *permanent* station—and where better than in the invigorating champagne-and-bloodstock atmosphere of Newmarket? In his modernization scheme the whole of the platform on one side of the line was to be transformed into the famous Long Odds Bar, scene of legendary Cesarewitch Night parties. But the technical side of racing was not to be ignored in favour of the social. Newmarket Station, the only one in the world with mounted porters, would become a favourite with bookmakers, who could stay in the Long Odds Bar, connected with their London offices by teleprinters (*pink* teleprinters) as an ingenious system of converted railways signals flagged results visibly to them from the famous course a few furlongs away.

It was this last that particularly enraged his chief opponent, Zoab Gridgeley, leader of the closure party. Gridgeley hated racing anyway. He once delivered an address to the annual conference of Grimmim Tosh (the sect also known as 'The Gloomy Brethren'), of which he was a leading figure, lashing out against the whole thing—the maddening pretty women in the ring after the wild exercise, the streaming manes and snorting nostrils, the unashamed joy in physical life. 'Woe unto them!' he thundered. 'Their stirrup-cups shall be dashed to the ground, and the harlot shall be dashed under their hooves. And he that maketh a book, his bowels shall be spilled upon the ground, nor shall it be given to men to know the beast and the running thereof, whether it be first or last, lest the eagle smite them with coals of fire and they become as dung.'

Gridgeley left school at 14, and worked his way up to the position of Head of Closure and Redundancy Branch after a career as Grease Devil, Firedropper, Yard Man, Top Link Man, Shunt Bogie Hand and Shed Master, improving himself by attendance at evening classes in double-entry book-keeping, Indian club drill and Hebrew. He came from a family well-known in railway restriction work; his great-grandfather was the famous 'Hubbub' Gridgeley prominent in the Victorian campaigns against Sunday trains.

d'Arcy-Poumphrey's race signals were filched from right under Gridgeley's nose, from one of his own closed lines; and of course this goaded him to fury. The moment he heard of it he burst into the Long Odds Bar, where the Colonel was the centre of an uproarious group of leather-faced men and proud, willowy girls.

' 'Tes nothin' but a heathen fandangle and a beastliness of Beelzebub,' he shouted, 'for to take the signs and marks of them as travelled godly and true on the good straight lines, an' to goo a-prostitewtin' an' a-fornicatin' of 'em with their jezebels an' their jeroboams!' His temper was not improved when the Colonel replied, 'Now Grudgeley, my dear fellow, you must not bear me a gridge.'

Gridgeley retired, his face working convulsively. But

d'Arcy-Poumphrey would have been well advised to tear himself away from Newmarket for a few days to see what his rival was up to at Divisional Headquarters, Norwich. As we all know, Zoab won his point. He plans to restore to the buildings their original cream and green paint, and to use them as a Mechanics' Institute and Teetotallers' Club for Young Railwaymen and Reformed Stable Lads. As for the long walk now necessary for passengers from taxis outside the closed gates of the Unmanned Halt, 'Why,' he says, with something close to a rusty smile, ' 'twill work the wickedness out o' the stiff-necked varmints of passengers with their worrits and complainin' and their godless waste of the paper towels.'

There are rumours, however, that d'Arcy-Poumphrey, far from accepting defeat, is now working on an ambitious and flamboyant scheme involving a double loop line from Newmarket station right round the racecourse, so that locomotive racing may alternate with the more conventional kind. This could well be another brilliant first, attracting large, mechanically-minded crowds from the cities as well as the usual racing people.

We shall see. Meanwhile, don't send any foals to Newmarket, or anything else. Like people, they will get an ambivalent reception from British Rail.

ℭ Ghosts: Reduce Speed

WHAT HAVE these names in common: Houghton Regis, Kidney Wood, Tingrith, Westoning, Milton Keynes, Moulsoe, Salcey Forest, Quinton Deanery, Floore, Barby, Ashby St Ledgers? Could a painstaking search of the map produce a list more evocative of the England that makes the very word *modernize* seem a bad joke? Tingrith, impenetrable pre-Saxon mystery—the Tingrith Ring, perhaps, a pattern of stones on some eerie knoll: fairies in a wood, flickering in the moonlight of Salcey Forest; folk-song so authentic that none of the rhymes are quite right:—

The Cheesemaker of Moulsoe
Courted a maid
For a year and a day
She took him for a fool, sir
With my nickety nackety niddle and noo, &c.

Lusty eighteenth-century horse racing by Squire Jack and his cronies (Ashby St Ledgers), pudding races at Floore, the Barby Oak Dance, a rooted earth-culture vaguely penetrated by mild parsons (Quinton Deanery), huzzas for a crown at Houghton Regis, high-domed Puritan intellectuals and organ music (Milton Keynes) ....

In fact this is just a random selection of the places within a mile or so of the M1. Those mysterious and untouchable fields that roll down to the soft shoulder, that mad suburban crest that one pierces (outcrop of Luton, would it be? Are there real women in those kitchens?). Those ponds, those strange dark woods that we can never enter—surely all this is exactly how the world appears, a kind of shadowy beige, to returned ghosts, who are in it but not of it? Surely we should understand and manage the M1 better if we admitted that it was *haunted*?

It is not the crude, obvious hauntedness of ghost stories. The mere costume ghost is utterly local, always in the same room or corridor. Doubtless any headless horseman riding the three miles from Nether to Harpole Hall (near Northampton) would resent now having to cross the M1, and possibly some of that fog confusion comes from local psychic eddies. It was much the same in the early days of railways. Mysterious single-line collisions like those at Thorpe (Norfolk) in 1874, or Radstock, in the Mendips, in 1876, involved inexplicable confusion in telegraph messages and the handing over of tokens, doubtless due to local ghosts. But the railways, infinitely solid, Victorian, prosaic, like tiny rows of bourgeois terraced houses moving along, soon grew out of this; they were only haunted, if at all, on the local level (all the action in *The Ghost Train* takes place at one station).

But on the M1 it is much more personal. We ourselves have got on to another, ghostly plane of reality, as matter becomes energy if you think quickly enough about it. We are tuned into strange emanations, drifts of the random ectoplasm of England. The M1, this great, literally concrete Thing, an object in the world if ever there was one, groaning and humming with millions of foot-pounds of real physical energy, real cars that have stood still in oily, matter-of-fact garages, nevertheless utterly detaches us from the present.

If we stop, it is as if at stations in some symbolic play. As in a dream, we ascend stairs, pass through glass doors. Mute servants move about with brushes, trays. A dreamy, not quite recognizable music tinkle-tonkles vaguely from the walls. Here, soundlessly speaking, are Two Women; an Old Man; a Family; Three Boys; a Man-and-Woman. We pass in a line, a Seated Woman scrutinizes us. The last time I stopped there was also a Rich Couple, he with grey topper, she in a floral hat, silently drinking coffee. One expected Michael Redgrave to come in, with some mist, as the Dead Pilot, and speak nobly to us. . . .

On the road itself, strange high nodding lorries materialize, lorries that you never see anywhere else. The names I wrote down after my last journey have the air of forgotten significance of any notes made after a receding dream. FARMERS MUSIC CIRCLE (serpents, shawms, old flutes, jigging in a commodious barn). FOLLOW THIS VAN FOR LONDON'S LARGEST SELECTION OF NEW AND SECOND-HAND OFFICE FURNITURE (suppose one did, could one ask the man when it finally stopped, down in E.1. somewhere, for a Victorian typewriter? Of course not. It *vanishes* at Watford). A huge lorry of rattling milk churns labelled simply KNIGHTS OF OLD. And most dreamlike of all, MOULDINGS, BOGNOR REGIS. LET US QUOTE YOU ANYWAY Mouldings? In *Bognor*? The words are wild. Our sea past, our literature (all right, quote us some Beowulf) and our industry are here assembled by the national subconscious in a momentary unity.

What the Ministry of Transport should do is put up huge signs every five miles saying BUT MOST OF IT IS REAL.

¢ The Neck Strine from Platform 2

✦✦✦

BETTER MEN than I have been fascinated by the idea of huge empty sunlit Australia (as unknown to the world until quite recently as his subconscious was to man) as a *symbolic* landscape—and I don't mean only painter S. Nolan. There was a review somewhere of *Voss*, by Patrick White (another great book I absolutely must read or I'll be seventy before I know where I am) lamenting the impossibility for an English novelist of making a journey inland from, say, Skegness (Lincs.) seem as symbolic as the great odyssey described in that universally praised Australian novel. And then there's the marvellous poem by D. H. Lawrence, about the kangaroo

She watches with insatiable wistfulness
Untold centuries of watching for something to come,
For a new signal from life, in that silent lost land of the South
Where nothing bites but insects and snakes and the sun, small life,
Where no bull roared, no cow ever lowed, no stag cried, no leopard screeched, no lion coughed, no dog barked,
But all was silent save for parrots occasionally, in the haunted blue bush.
Wistfully watching, with wonderful liquid eyes.
And all her weight, all her blood, dripping sack-wise down towards the earth's centre....

It's impossible not to feel that the Australians, now they have come, are making up for lost time, their shouts echo across that huge continent; how like us, with their drinking hours and cricket and awful cooking, and the sacred 'smoko', equivalent to our tea-break—and yet how unlike, in their relaxed openness!

Until I actually do read *Voss*, and probably even after, my chief imaginative short cut to the otherness of Australia is going to be the 1959 timetable of the Western Australian Government Railways. It's been on my desk since 1959 because I seem to be using it as a file, and scarcely a day passes without a subliminal glance at some such place-name as Karrakatta or Cowcowing or Winceballup.

Don't misunderstand me. I know it's perfectly simple to look more closely and see that Karrakatta is thirteen minutes from Perth on the short suburban line to Fremantle, and is probably about as other as Notting Hill Gate. Yet even *our* station names do mysteriously tell you some basic truth about England, if you have ears to listen. Is there not something of Milton and Bunyan about that very Notting Hill Gate line, where you progress biblically through the *Marble Arch* to *Shepherd's Bush* and the ultimate, shining *White City*? Does not the Piccadilly Line recall heraldic medieval and Shakespearean wars—*Baron's Court, Earl's Court, Gloucester Road, Knightsbridge, Leicester Square, King's Cross*?

But all this is buried under layers of old time and sooty brick. The point about my WA timetable is that here, for those of us who have never seen this dreamlike land and are likely to remain in our complex, subdivided, windswept, many-roofed, art-groaning European towns for the rest of our lives, are names with a direct and sunlit freshness which must surely convey a poetically true vision of Australia.

The overwhelming impression is one of jovial sociability. Obviously the sight of a fellow human being at such places, nakedly functional in the vast emptiness, as *Toolibin, Thirty Mile Peg* or *Kronkup Turnoff* is one to quicken the heart, and perhaps to give rise to a long, semi-ritual conversation, a *Gabbin* or *Gabalong.* It would be nice to think that the aborigines do this too, that whereas one goes 'walkabout' on one's own, one goes *gabalong* with a companion.

This was the basic pioneering situation, but during the nineteenth century, as towns and settlements grew, this fundamental sociability found reflection in numerous social holidays which centred very much round the horse and horse-racing. Perhaps *Gwindinnup, Gwambygine, Jerramungup* and *Gidgiegannup* were named after the actual cries with which the drivers of four-in-hands and buggies, streaming out in gay family parties to the races, urged on their horses.

The Irish, needless to say, were very prominent in all this. What should the racecourse itself be called but *Donnybrook*? And it is easy to imagine the colourful scene under that fluttering Victorian bunting, shining with the innocence of a primitive painting in a foreground of green grass, with distant views of eucalyptus and spinifex, single or in clumps, fading into far-off blue hills, with unknown desert behind them. One can hear the odds being shouted: *Seven to one Mullalyup, Manjimup, Boyup! Chorkerup,* Charlie' (this last to the bookmaker's clerk). 'Man Jim' is a name that has all the symbolic overtones of Ned Kelly, and if there aren't legends about his prowess as a jockey, even though handicapped by weight (for Man Jim, surely, was no stripling), it's time there were.

After the races, particularly those near the towns with their womenfolk and settled family life, there would be some kind of enormous feast, a *Wellbungin,* perhaps, or a *Bungulluping*. Indeed, even in the Australia of those days there may have been some fragmentary beginning of that urban ennui and discontent that runs through America today, when instead of an infinite, vague land to the west, a fluid and adventurous frontier region, all they have is Los Angeles, as municipal as Nuneaton; and tough, bearded bushwhackers, regarding such a bourgeois function with incredulous scorn written all over their leathery features, would refer to it as a *Yabberup*, fit only for a lot of *Nambling* milksops and Poms.

Many such, like the roving heroes of *The Summer of the Seventeenth Doll,* would put off settling down to such faintly shameful domesticity (in a *Dwellingup*) until well into middle age. For them, even at such outlandish stations as *Wungong,* where the single general store, run by a Chinaman, was the only place for off-duty relaxation, the great weekend function would be the *Noggerup*—or, not infrequently, the more boisterous and violent *Gingin.* One may easily imagine the rivalry caused in the tension of enforced male continence by the appearance of a rare single woman—such a one as the famous *Wilga Turnoff,* with her smouldering Slavonic eyes, brought to these outposts by who knows what nineteenth-century tale of oppression and escape and wandering. Her arrival would be quite enough to turn a *Gingin* into a *Punchmirup* . . .

Ah, legendary days! I daresay it's not at all like that now. All the same, I'm pretty sure that a place like *Damboring* is not in the least what such a name would imply in England.

WORD WORDS

₡ Say it in Minglish

(An editorial from the *European Times*, circa 2010)

✦✦✦

ON HET thirtieht anniversar of the funding of hte Unitted Slates of Europ, greelings to all our reabers! All-person yong and anctient can look mit prid satisfactioun on the extroardinar vapid developpment of Minglish in to a mihgtig, flexile langage, easy beknowed to evrye constitung-poeple of Europp, wether it's matrix-tong was Italien, Franch, Duetsche or Anglish.

A vash, inopible tasking! A lingistic feet to mesh the braines of mastrephilologes! So mihgt spake such non-credent cyniqes of htirty annes agone. Und also treu migt be such prognostic if that operating, to froge a glossar-universel of Evropean—putt in our head the versating Labor-dozen of Herkule!—was left to Academes! You may image it! Wat strifings, wat inter-mined commissions having discution, wat argusment, prehaps coming to blobs and strike!

We scrate in elder, dusted file-journales of France in such bypass daies, and find the scolar-puristic by every-were nevrose at such-called intrudels of *weekend, dancing, le steam-cracking, la manpowerization* and many varigal ensemples of Franglaise. Hola, mann the barbicade and save-honor the pureness-clarety of smother-tong, crie scolardy Docteurs! And by this also, how shuold the German sprake wich have crafig declinings be mongled with the analytice, oddsome, unsyn-netrcicale Englis word? Morever pandits could bong their heads togather over like prodlematic, e.g. contra-punct of Englihs iambich-rhythm and the musicale tenderose female-ending, all troochhee-meter, by Italiano. How by devils-name can any lerning enrond sich a pangloss?

Butt, neverstanding that Anglis-saxony posse a mundial spread, in U.S.A. nort-american landes and Australantipods, also for comercials in Afrique trade, such a fearing it wuold impermate Enrope as jugglernaut, did swaftly proved a fools vaine, a chimeara of the intelligents.

For by all this so, its to ken by each person that our gloried Minglish universal-sprak is distinted quite O.K. from English-tong. Und why? To response is that in each terran, Spanien and Turc, Griesch too, outlands also in Communmarkt landes, were fecundating in each resort, each panoram-delihgt, evry beauty-spo and thermale heath-plage or turist ruines of classics-tempel, grand daedal printers and auctors to guide boolets and turismo-informats. In such volcan-forg was the nice precis and lingafranc litter bonked, wich now bibble on the lip of childs from Bremen to Naple, in total areage of our Continental.

So *Hopp*! it cried to professeur with bibliotek of lexicons and comparing interglossals to make from abstruct a Eorupemann's lingage. Be gone, mit all porings and schema from grammatiques wich run only in your heads! Here in pangraphic stile of brochure-leafs, and so of hotels-pubblicite, and noticaments to foreingturistes in very nice vacacion sitts, here is new speaching-grund for conversating of all euRopeen gentrys.

No Englander, natal of such locale as Warington, Botle, Noneatun, Bis Hopstorfod or Londre himselve can say wit his poete Walther Scotch 'this is my owl, my dative tong'; as by seen anterior, Minglish is no Inglesh. Yet as thought by hug sobterranic forze, such a wording cognat to each turist from Amerik also and inteligent to all, bumped into existence fulsy maturn like Athena born. Miraculose of Europ psycheal! Grand fork of inspiration! Instant commune deal! As if by wading of magics wind, humbel and obscure writers of spa programs, menu traductions, public-affiches and museo-guibes from Hellsinki to Sicel hat on the same herbal felicitie, the same convortion and distinged matter.

Yet truely, wen we make a stopp to bark this phenomenal, we arene't amuzed. Is it not by the commune tramping of grandiflored meals, by grande prospekt on sin-glozed beeches on Mediterran vacacion, by the ambiance-turist of her bushing citys and typical cathedrales that we have our hearting of Europa? Lingist is to yomp from experiment-realitat; and fuller hoppiest realitey of manskind is not in the shouling clamant of the markt-place and diurne laboring. Never such! It is spirting in the foomy wavelets, it is sunbashing in the tronquil baie, it is maiestic panoram from alpin-telepherique where his soul burst and wander.

And wider, a noval face of this self-forme uttering of Minglish litters is, you can uniquely deviate its orthograph to your voluntary. Which nobile complexity, to have such varies, to fit like fingers in your globe!

So is to reflexion the spewing aspects, like a million, of our continente; the grand porphyreal tumbs and billowed colonnades, the pintured gravity of the maestral renascimento of Italy! The somptuous edificacion and enlightened avenues of Paris, where you may see artist in his smack at work to strain the trembling coloures of the *ville lumière*! Or you could spun throuht its smiting paysage of fairies châteaux nodding their dreames by the Loire to the bostling chic of the Cote d'Azur, and busk in sinshine. Or you can cure athmsma and hyper-nevrose febrile at thermal balneic station, first class. Than you can gear to redonded curvature of Baroc-stil and onion-doms in a little valle of Bavaria. Hisht! You have nought to hear but tinkel-bells of a cow mooching near. Now you see yong pople in a quant rustique dress jangle and lep in a folklortypic dance from two hundred years. Now you blow your breath to inspice a grandly frawning vista from the mihgty Alpes.

All such divers, but yet its too a bee-hove commercial manufactory and negotiant communite. You can't expect it, how she pulsate, each time a change, so we could match Euorupes complice trails of strand with this pusty, varigous, fluvent now-speech, the same wen you watch alwaies, yet never lagged by the binds of a wrotten orthograph-grammatical—our nobile, mobile tong of Minglish.

¢ Accustomed as it is

(If a computer did the Royal Christmas message)

++

CHRISTMAS NATIVITY Yule Xmas Joy Merry Greetings Goodwill Hooray Cheer Rhubarb testing testing.

CORRECTION Noel Noel Noel Good King Wenceslas good king queen ace jack.

RE-SET QUEEN message follows

QUEEN wish all objects

CORRECTION queen wish all SUBJECTS loyal subjects Hippy Chrastmas

CORRECTION Heppy Crossmas Crossman QUERY goodwill no cross man all jolly CORRECTION HAPPY CHRISTMAS

All peopl at this time recall peace PROTEST

RE-SET peace PROTEST VIETNAM

RE-SET PEACE PEACE PEACE all people at this time recall PEACE first Christmas.

QUERY ALL QUERY check stastical unit

Latest figures 21 twentyone percent, believe first Christmas GOD made man 37 thirtyseven percent atheist NONGOD 33 thirtythree percent jews mohammedans swedenborgians RE-SET 21 twentyone percent people at this time recall PEACE first Christmas message agricultural labourers

CHECK VOCAB UNIT obsolete agricultural labourers hedger ditcher milkmaid drover shepherd ACCEPT shepherd SHEPHERD

RE-SET QUEEN message follows 21 twentyone percent people at this time recall PEACE first Christmas message SHEPHERDS heard from angels

CHECK OBSOLETE VOCAB ANGELS QUERY demiurges fairies spirits naiads CHERUBIM SERAPHIM THRONES POWERS DOMINATIONS HOSANNA HOORAY GOODWILL

QUERY angels SPACE MESSENGERS QUERY

But whatever belief my people O my People O my People at this time we ALL ALL ALL think of family renewal family life home children CHECK STATISTI-CATSICS UNIT latest figures 27 twentyseven percent. Christmas NOT AT HOME further 11 eleven percent would go away if could afford TORQUAY BRIGHTON IMPERIAL HOTELS booked

But whatever belief

RE-SET QUEEN message follows whatever belief whether family circle or wearing funny HATS BRIGHTON hotel or field mine workshop fight on beaches BRIGHTON those who serve community essential public service

Query DUSTMEN STRIKE QUERY

CANCEL QUERY this IS Christmas lolly jelly jollybox compliments of season CANCEL DUSTMEN QUERY

RE-SET QUEEN O ALL PEOPLE whatever belief this time great change decimal system HEPTAGONAL tenshilling new role BRITain EUROPe common-WEALTH euROPE COMMonWEALTH EuRope COMMONWEALTH EUROPE seesaw margery daw

CHECK STISTASTIC UNIT

STASTITIC

STASTISTICC ACCEPT STASTISTICC UNIT latest figures 34 thirtyfour percent for Europe 33.9 thirtythreepointnine against 999999999 dont know O ALL BRITISH people whatever belief future IS WITH youth new ROLE Britain YOUth and all who serve in IT special thought those youth at HEART this time hippy HOPPY heppy hap per PERHAPPY XYZMAS

21 twentyone percent. GOD save all of us happy merry holly berry message end 999999999

ℂ Penguin Fictionary

I ALWAYS HAD a faint suspicion that the compilers of my edition of the *Encyclopaedia Britannica* did a little juggling to get resonant-sounding titles for each volume —SHUVA to TOMTOM, REFEC to SHUTT and, best of all, LORD to MUMPS, which seems in one phrase to embrace all the splendours and miseries of the human condition.

But after looking at the page-headings of the new *Penguin Dictionary* I see this is something our language achieves by itself in a marvellous kind of spontaneous generation; related words join up automatically, new concepts germinate before your eyes. Some could go straight into the language, like *vinegar-plant-virtuous* or *letter-box-libellous*; and I am sure there must actually *be* something called *frizz-fructose,* some kind of frightful synthetic fruit omelette eaten in the kind of neon-lit snack bar where you go when there is not time for a sit-down meal before a theatre.

These first-and-last words on each page give a rich, associative and exact picture of the present state of our civilization. It is no good being *vinegar-plant-virtuous* or *smug-sniff* about the *affluence-age-group*. Any *reach-me-down-realist* could tell you we live in an age of crumbling values, surrounded on all sides by *fair-false-faced* prophets; and many is the *febrile-fellow* who would offer us a *false-hearted-fantasia.*

Many seek refuge in material distractions, they take solace in *butterfly-by-products,* status symbols—some flashy gimcrack boat, perhaps, with *celluloid-centre-board*, in which they can show off, endlessly *voyage-*

vying in the game of *beggar-my-neighbour-bell-buoy*. They never actually do real sailing in the boats. With a landlubber's *catfish-caution* they stay in *port-possession*; not for them the *bulkhead-bump* and *scuffle-sea-legs* of a real *regatta-rehearsal*. No, all one sees is the *pale-paunch swim-suit-sybarite,* the weekender with a motor cruiser trying to pick up girls. Many a *colleen-colourable,* in her *chatty-chemise,* is reduced to *blushing-bobbery* by his wolf-whistles and *louche* cries of *attaboy-auburn*! She would do well to steer clear of men with such *consumable-continence* and remember that the *callbox-camellia* is simply the prelude to a *joystick-jump,* and that the life of the *adulteress-aerial* is not without its risks of *courtly-cowpox*. And even if the affair results in marriage, too soon the loved one becomes a mere *haggish-half-and-half,* an unromantic *girdle-Glauber's salt* figure.

Instead of a sober, industrious population working away at *bobbin-boiling, clicker-clockwork* and other profitable export trades, we have a *baksheesh-balmy* welfare state full of idlers intent on trivial diversions like *nib-ninepins* and *nineteen-nod,* a nation of mere sport heroes like *grab-greaves* and *goalie-golden-rod* and living in a state of permanent *half-back-hallucinosis*.

Constant staring at television with its tendency to *maypole-mechanize* pleasure, has made them easy meat for routine, *imitator-immutable* shows, the *sting-ray-stock rider* soap-operas cooked up by the *scourge-screen-writer,* not to mention the cheapjack advertisers, *silkily-sincere,* offering their *whiteness-wideawake worldliness-wrapper*.

There is *feud-fiduciary* class war between the people and the *Etonian-evasive, grill-room-growl, enslave-entrepreneur*. In home politics even the *bumper-*

bureaucrat or the politician with his *quinquennium-quotient,* seems unable to stop the disease of the lightning *strawberry-strike;* and he may be forced to be both *prohibitive-prompt* and *press-gang-preventive.* In foreign policy both our *orbicular-Orient* and *wop-world* plans have come to nothing, and we seem to be just a *subatomic-sublessor* of America—and goodness knows they have their own troubles there, with many a *congressman-conscience-smitten.*

Science, with the *stopcock-strabismus* producing his *quantum-queer thermion-thing,* has forced us into a crisis in religious thought, a real *prebendary-predicament,* which the work of people like the Bishop of Woolwich and much *ill-timed-imitative* writing showing *alto-ambivalence* to traditional Christian ideas has done nothing to relieve (although received with *éclat-editorial*). Obviously, mere local, *lugger-Lutheran* or *vernacular-vestryman* religion will have to be replaced by something worldwide, embracing all mankind (including the *orbicular-Orient*!); even *panacea-papalism* may not be a wide enough concept for this new universal religion, a kind of *koala-kyrie-eleison.*

One thing is certain. It's no good looking down the *nostalgia-nozzle.* We must take our *frail-free* destinies in our own hands and get really *thingummy-thoughtful.*

IMAGINARY WORDS

ℂ The Curse of the Hoteleks

✦✦

SURELY A science-fantasy novel could be written (instead of which it's got to fit into 750 words, as usual) in which the human race is taken over and utterly enslaved by ruthless, cold-eyed mutants; unsuspected, they build their own establishments in our very midst, until, one day, these outnumber our own houses. One morning *everybody* will just happen to be staying in all these proliferating hotels, and then—*pffff*! Doors will close noiselessly, and from the grandest Hilton to the scruffiest White Lion we shall all be prisoners of the dreaded Hoteleks.

Those men with unplaceable foreign accents, in black coats and striped trousers, behind the reception grilles; those waiters kicking open service doors and whispering tight-lipped messages of hate to one another; those silent women who always happen to be walking past our bedroom door when we come out (they carry piles of sheets, or abstractedly polish some rail, or speak into an unnatural-looking telephone); those pert, prematurely old boys—*they* will give the orders then.

Take the male human beings to the dining room, a metallic voice, hideously magnified, will screech from those little radio outlets in a hundred thousand bedrooms with floral carpets, wash-basins, too-high beds, unconvincing little tables. And suddenly we shall all realize, what they have known for months in a Whitehall where telephones now shrill uselessly in deserted offices—that all those old forts and ships off Essex are the command centres of the Hoteleks.

For months there have been anxious secret conferences. 'I tell you, Chief of Staff, the people are getting restless. We've had this secret B.B.C. station pumping out pop music, we've put out this story about some young Irishman running it from a boat, rumours of an international consortium, mysterious Swiss bankers and the rest of it. But people are asking why the Navy . . .'

The Admiral, who has been staring through the window out over doomed London, turns round wearily. He is holding a slip of paper. 'I've just had this signal, Postmaster-General,' he says harshly. 'Two frigates with the new electronic screening got to within five miles of *Queen of the Pops* last night. I don't know what those damnable Hoteleks used, but a helicopter that managed to keep out of range reports that both ships *simply seemed to disintegrate.* No fire or anything, they just fell apart.' He pauses slightly. 'My son was in command of one of them . . .'

One hears bursts of tinny pop from teenagers' handbags, but it's only in hotel bedrooms, when one is alone, that the full, well, *disjointedness* of it is apparent. The Hoteleks, trying to tune in to the warm rhythms of human life, its music, speech and entertainment, achieve only a frightful cold mateyness which ought to deceive no one.

There isn't actually so *much* pop and beat on hotel bedroom radios as you get from the teenagers' handbags. But every time you switch to a different segment of the little wall panel the programme that was there before has altered, there is an inhuman absence of continuity. The Hotelek broadcasters impersonate shop stewards in obscure industrial rows ('we asked Ron Herbage to explain the Wedge Picklers' position') and other people in fringe news stories.

The actual music requests ('for Stanley Cakeface, Josie Paloosa and her friend Elkin,' I heard a Hotelek announcer say scornfully) are mostly like Muzak only louder—all voluptuous echoing strings, devil-drumming and shouting, with a vaguely thirties feeling, as though they hadn't got our time-scale quite right; it seems to come from some hellish disembodied cinema bathed in red and green light. And I absolutely swear I heard a Hotelek say, 'Hello there, Alice, this is for you; *I left my aunt in San Francisco*.'

Then a male voice began to sing, with infinite sadness,

I left my aunt in San Francisco
High on a hill she called to me
Where liddle cable cars
Climb halfway to the stars.

In any other context this would have a real human pathos. One would see the little apple-cheeked Aunt—Aunt Maybelle—who had brought up the singer orphaned as a boy of six, the Sunday dinners with blueberry pie, brought in by the Aunt in checked gingham; the tears bravely checked when the growing lad went away to college, his successful legal career in San Francisco, the timid appearance of the Aunt at a smart party on a patio overlooking the Golden Gate, his rejection of her, his subsequent flight from his artificial life, his remorse, the search for the lost Aunt. . . .

But coming from the Hoteleks it seems, like everything they do, much more sinister and unnatural. Watch out.

ℂ Lift up Your Herts

IT GIVES one a great sense of the mystery of life to go, as I sometimes do, from Bishop's Stortford to Aylesbury. This is simply the middle stretch of a journey from East Bergholt to Oxford, or Paignton, or Cardiff, or some such place. The two outer stretches—East Bergholt to Bishop's Stortford and Aylesbury to wherever-it-is—are just bits of England; parkland, wolds, churches behind trees; police cars, pubs, towns becoming informal with children at 4 p.m.; blond gentlemen farmers in Land Rovers; Atlantic clouds, a people dreaming behind a million front doors.

That middle part, Hertfordshire, secret shut-in fields and dark little towns, that's where Chesterton's Secret People live, in an England older and newer than can ever be written about. The New Towns, De Havillands, jet aircraft, mysterious factories in fields, these are an advanced intellect, a final articulation, a super-ego sitting above the great id of London and subsuming it. But all those little dark villages and hedges and little low houses, those silent-bustling towns with many yards containing enormous blank high wooden buildings, are an ancient secret compared with which St Alban's Cathedral, or the church at Tewin (named after Tew, the Saxon god of war, like Tuesday), is as new as the jets.

One day a hundred Hertfordshire men—technicians in white coats, peasants with walnut-tree complexions, publicans, horsemen, tennis players, wild Saxons, quiet deacons—will come marching down through Edgware, Watford, Harrow, Willesden, gathering huge crowds with unanswerable words, and all will be changed. 'Yes, that's it, of course,' we shall say. '*That's* what they've been working out all this time, no wonder they haven't had time to impose a form on Hertfordshire if they've been working on that.'

Even by car one can get only an inkling of it, on this east-west journey that the whole map and landscape warn against. Railways and main roads ignore it, as they are meant to, pushing north from London to other matter-of-fact places. One slips through these vertical bamboo thickets in a jungle and sees concealed clearings.

No wonder these tight, anonymous towns and villages have the air of being named temporarily, with any old slinging together of basic place-name syllables like *den, stead, ham, field, bury*. Thus they have Hertingfordbury, Sawbridgeworth, Bayfordbury, Gaddesden, Hoddesdon, Wheathampstead, Hemel Hempstead, *two* Berkhamsteds, Hatfield. You feel they might just as well have said Hatfieldbury, Sawhampstead, Gadfieldbury, Berkenden, Hatbridgefieldworthbury. It's all the same to them. They leave it to Luton or Dunmow to be ordinary, individual towns, with settled names. In Hertfordshire all is in a mysterious flux. All unobserved, they are turning the twentieth century to England's account, they are supplying material for Trends before anyone actually starts writing about them.

And lest anyone imagine that all this is purely subjective, let me add that not long ago, trying to get across this county by yet another route, I saw with my own eyes, outlined against a vast Atlantic sunset, three workmen dancing on top of a gasometer in Stevenage; a bergomask, or could it have been a gasomask?

I do not want to know what good fortune was the cause of their dancing—the birth of a fine boy, a pools-win or pay-rise, or perhaps just a sudden access of joy up there in the flaming sky above the crawling earth-bound traffic, something *given*, divine. But I do not think any other county could claim this. In a way you could say that a gasometer is the opposite of a dance; it is so big and serious. Dancing and gasometers can be brought together only in the surrealist country where opposites are resolved—in Hertfordshire, ultra-rural and ultra-urban, old and new, London and not-London.

In the most secret part of all there is a river with a surrealist name that seems to have come straight out of Lewis Carroll; for it is called, believe it or not, the *Mimram*; and I should like to think that those gasmen, as well as dancing, were singing, or lewiscarrolling, this runic Hertfordshire song:—

> *Millhillig, gas for lightly stoves*
> *To ware and hemel in the globe:*
> *South mimmsy are the borough groves*
> *And the home radlett probe.*
> *Mimram, broxbourne, potters bar*
> *We sing and royston all in parts*
> *Ware is tring and further far*
> *And barnet burble in our herts.*
> Chorus: *Mim, ram, bim, bam,*
> *Gasmen hertsmen here we am.*

But no Hertfordshire man will ever betray the secret of the tune.

Ideal Weather

I REMEMBER READING in 1933, when I was in the fifth form, in a feature called *Piccalilli (by The Pickler)* in the *Sunday Express* (it may be there still for all I know), that 1922 had been a good summer, so had 1911. They came every eleven years.

I thought, as I go through life I will look out for this. I can't speak for 1944, I was in India; it was very hot, it is true, but of course it doesn't count there. 1955, if you remember, *was* good, so there's hope for us all, and by golly I need it on the bitter May day (with thunderstorms; cold thunderstorms; when I was a boy you only had thunder after heatwaves) when I am actually writing this piece. But deep down I know, I think we all know, that the perfect, languorous, endless hot summer that we all dream of had very much better remain a dream.

I wouldn't go as far as Kingsley, who *liked* it cold—

Let the luscious South-wind
Breathe in lovers' sighs,
While the lazy gallants
Bask in ladies' eyes.
What does he but soften
Heart alike and pen?
'Tis the hard gray weather
Breeds hard English men . . .

(Unlike me, Kingsley never had to play hockey against Pakistanis, or Indians, as they were then called; I'd like to hear him recite that, in goal, with three of them coming at him who'd never seen a day of hard grey weather in their lives.) I can't speak for Fisher and Ludlow panel-beaters, who walked out on a hot day recently, or people trapped inside the burning-glasses that all modern office blocks become when, to the astonishment of their 'architects', it is hot in London; but I myself can work better when it's hot. The only thing that spoils it for me is when, after a long spell of such work, I say to a shop assistant or bus conductor, 'Isn't it marvellous,' and *they* say darkly, 'Oh, it's all right if you haven't got to work,' as though I were some kind of plantation-owner.

All the same, there is something vaguely comforting about this eleven-year thing. On the one hand it's encouraging to know that one will at least have six good summers during the allotted life-span: and on the other that lurking fear that unless it keeps fairly nippy we shall become decadent is kept at bay. You've only got to read an abridgment of the abridged Toynbee to see that the general picture of civilizations is of gentle thin-wristed people in the sun, with priests who could foretell eclipses and do quadratic equations, and goldsmiths making tinkling ornaments for princesses in cool palaces overlooking shimmering seas, progressively overcome by red-bearded thugs from some howling waste to the north full of cold dust-clouds (and, by the time it was our turn, cold thunderstorms in May). I don't know why we're all so worried about the Russians (the Black Sea ones, anyway) and the Chinese; it's the Eskimos we ought to be watching.

After all, it's bound to happen in 70 million years. That's the time it has taken us to get from the Ice Age to what is laughingly called Temperate, so if we go on like this (and here I am only extrapolating, like any other scientist), in another 70 million we shall be Tropical.

It will be different then. In the First Tropical Period most of the country will be covered with impenetrable rain forests and a Burmese-type jungle, at the heart of which slumber torpid towns fainting in the humid heat (nine months of it, followed by three months' ceaseless rain); towns like Bir Min Gham, She Rin Gham (a coastal settlement, this one, houses on stilts of teak and mahogany reaching out into the shallow blue sea, not far from the spice trading post of Crom Er). The nominal capital of this largely unexplored country will be Cre We, two days' overland journey from the canoe staging-point of Wid Nes. Travellers will have made the journey up the muddy, crocodile-infested creek from Boo Tle, with its ramshackle hotel on the wooden verandah of which traders, explorers and the odd archaeologist sip their drinks, read their mail and pray for a slight breeze from the leaden sea.

Traces of an earlier civilization (earlier by a mere 1,000 years or so) will remain in two towns huddled round the remains of enormous monasteries, Tha Me and Tha Tcham, and the mysterious Holy City of Mu Chha Dham. There will be articles in learned Polynesian journals, with titles such as *The Sto Towns of Britain: Pre-Tropical or Temperate?* These will refer to ruins, thought to be fortified sites, like Sto-Kepo Ges, Sto Nystra Tton, and the recently unearthed Sto Wmark Et. The wildest and least explored part will be a large hilly area in the north-west known as the Ri Pon, mostly inaccessible by river and swarming with head-hunters.

In the Second Tropical Period, some million years later, this period will itself be the subject of vague archaeological conjecture. Britain will now be of great importance, for all its backward, unruly tribal politics, as a main source of oil and methane for internal combustion engines, now rediscovered some two hundred years. Major powers (Greenland, Antarctica, Japan) will fight for concessions; but for the men who work the wells it will be a tough life. El Y will be famous as 'the hottest spot on earth', and life at the big methane centres like Hal-i-fax, El Tham, Aru N'del and Fareh Am will be mainly for tough, hard-drinking bachelors who sweat it out in three-month stints, although later a few families will appear, as new, air-conditioned townships are built on blinding, treeless salt flats like the Da Tchet and the Uttox Eter.

But the political set-up will be tense and uneasy. The traditional ruler, the Ney, will scarcely exert any authority outside his crumbling palace in the ancient capital of his line, Ol Ney, in spite of massive subventions of Greenland money. The armies of his chief rebel opponent will sally out unchecked from their lair at Ched Dar, two days' hard riding across the desert; the massive fortress built into the rock at Ched Dar will be virtually impregnable. To the east a wild religious fanatic, Pelesok, from his stockaded camp at Thor Pelesok En (not unaided by Japanese money, some will say) will terrorize the coastal districts, ambushing parties of the Ney's Government troops and cutting pipelines. Nor will the brand new university put up with Antarctican money at Al Dershot prove anything but an embarrassment to its sponsors as its rioting students set yet another installation on fire . . .

The thing is, no inhabitants, in either of these periods, will do any real *work,* resulting in a hard currency and a dominant position. It's better the way we are now, surely: only like this every eleven years?

¢ But Don't Pull it over Your Eyes

Now that everyone's on about circulation and manning problems in Fleet Street I can't think why we don't hear more about the inmost in-term of all, the C.T.W. of a journal. Admittedly I've just invented it, but now I've done it, it instantly has an objective, classical look, like B.T.U. (oh, *come* on, British Thermal Unit) or M.P.H. or, I was just going to say, L.S.D. (which is always going to mean good old money to me; I'm too old even to want to work out the derivation of *psychedelic*). 'C.T.W.' stands for an absolutely basic concept in modern journalism, *Cost per Thousand Women.*

You've only got to look through any specialist publication of the advertising world, directed at those stony space-buyers who hold in their hands the whole future of the printed word outside mere books, to see how they bandy C.T.W. about. There are one or two half-hearted claims by the tosh—sorry, *posh* papers, to have all the wealthy AB readers; or (by papers which to be seen with marks you as culturally CDE) claims that CDE is the mass market anyway. But you can tell their heart isn't in it. It's these bundles of a thousand women they're really interested in, that's when their eyes light up as if they were Circassian slavemasters.

It's not surprising that if papers like the *Daily Mirror,* in an ad headed 'FULLY FASHIONED' and showing some girls' legs, says *The Mirror's low cost per thousand women fits the needs of fashion perfectly,* etc., actual *women's* papers feel they have to shout even louder. And this leads me to my favourite ad for a long time. It says *If all the readers of one issue of 'Woman's*

Own' were each to knit a sweater they'd use more than 3,171 tons of wool.

Under that, a conscientious afterthought in smaller print, it says *allowing 16 ozs.* (surely they mean 16 oz.?) *of wool per garment.* And under that, in large, confident letters, it says *7,105,000 women readers. 6/4 a page a thousand.*

It's all right as far as it goes, as British Railways say when they close another line. I'm sure they *have* got 7,105,000 readers, and they're right about its being more than 3,171 tons, I've worked it out, it's 3,171·875 tons. But I'm also sure that anyone seeing this ad must sense a discrepancy between the words, the very idea of these vast but cheaply bought throngs of women, the great cargo of wool, and the artwork (as we call it), which is a gentle, against-the-light photograph of the hands of *one* woman (·0000107d. per page to get her, I make it) knitting from an ordinary ball of wool.

One does not need to be the advertising manager of *Woman's Own* to long for some kind of physical realization of this enormous concept. Once you've actually written it down, *3,171 tons of wool,* it already has existence, at least as much as the God of St Anselm's proof has existence (he said God is the biggest *existing* reality you can think of, therefore He exists; but let's not go into that just now).

I myself see it brought specially from Australia (it is a nice soft merino wool) in a special boat. I'm not very well up in the relationship between a ship's weight and its cargo, but from the way a quite small piece of soap can sink my children's plastic jobs in the bath I should have thought you'd need something in the 8—10,000 ton range to carry 3,171 tons of wool.

So there is this great ship (the *Dame Nellie Melba,*

Fremantle, 9,000 tons) at Southampton. The moment she is berthed and the gangway lowered three Englishmen go up it with briefcases and papers. Two of them are officials with Bills of Lading, Loading Notes, Letters of Ullage, Manifest Sheets, Commission Release Bonds, Hull Equal Charge Claims, Port Dockets, Demand and Release Papers, Tax Differential Slips, Bottomry Vouchers, P. 104s and the rest of it. The third goes straight up to the Captain.

'I'm the *Woman's Own* man,' he says.

Lean, tanned Captain Herb Kelly runs a hand over his bristly chin. 'Stone the crows,' he says, 'I don't know how you Poms do it. Got any spare ones? Me and my cobbers been at sea for four lahsy weeks in this tub.'

'I've got 7,105,000,' says the WO man, and the misunderstanding is laughingly explained. But when the first hatch is lifted he is dismayed to find that instead of 7,105,000 x 16, that is 113,680,000 little 1 oz. balls, it is one enormous, continuous length (I haven't worked *that* out, but 7 million miles of it wouldn't surprise me, when you think how much there is in an ounce).

The original, already cumbrous plan had been to give away a pound of wool to each reader, but this is now clearly impossible. Slowly a beautiful, terrible idea dawns on the two men. It is the Australian who expresses it first. 'Why,' he says, 'don't you get those bloody sheilas to make the biggest bloody sweater in the bloody world?'

It is an idea impossible to dismiss, and it instantly seizes the imagination of the 7,105,000 women. Hitherto the only drawback about knitting, that basic female urge to make more and more soft woollen things, has been its solitary character; but this is social knitting.

Special trains from all over England (each holding a thousand women, so that British Railways can boast about their C.T.W. as well) come to Southampton, and fleets of buses take them the rest of the way to the clearing in the New Forest to which the wool is winched straight from the *Dame Nellie Melba* by a kind of overhead railway. The knitting is on a slatted floor raised ten feet above the ground and extended as work proceeds; the women knit in long lines, chattering and laughing on stilts, like the old hop pickers. *Woman's Own* helicopters buzz over the busy scene, there are canteens, rest-rooms, a hotel with viewing balcony for foreign visitors . . .

As the vast garment (about 2 square miles, I make it) grows there is increasing argument about its future. Put it on a huge female figure visible 50 miles out to sea, a kind of English Statue of Liberty? Spray it with lacquer and use it as a tremendous car-park roof? Fit it with buoyancy tanks and tow it back to Australia? Whatever they do, it doesn't seem likely to help them towards the goal of modern journalism—keeping the C.T.W. down.

ℭ Bad Antimony Drives out Good

COULD IT be that 'a technique of exporting' is a contradiction in terms, that you can't plan it just like that? Whenever one reads about some big export achievement it has a quality of divine surprise, accident, chance. A teenage girl goes to New York, apparently just for fun, and suddenly there are these tough buyers from big stores, women with rhinestone spectacles, falling over themselves to buy a million pairs of red felt stockings from her workshop, an attic in King's Road; some advertising figure—a man with a beard, or an eye-patch—achieves an unpredictable folklore status; British pop becomes actually cruder than American pop, and therefore exportable. You can't plan this kind of thing.

When it comes to the big stuff, if it's good enough it exports itself. Those Japanese shipbuilders didn't go to P. & O.; P. & O. went to them. If you manufacture, say, Jolt Squeeze Rollover and Pin Lift Moulding Machines (and people do), or Double-Headed Semi-Automatic Flat Ware Machines and Batt Cutters ('no wet-faced batts, less trouble with slurry marks,' says the leaflet before me), you are up against either countries which make perfectly good Jolt Squeeze Rollover and Pin Lift Machines of their own (and, quite possibly, *entirely* automatic Batt Cutters), or countries full of bamboo and a thousand twangling instruments, where they're just not interested.

Actual export managers, of firms making things like toys, servo-couplings, filing systems, patent roofing materials, are citizens of a realm of chance, quirk, otherness. With drip-dry shirts and workmanlike luggage in a dozen countries they go to patio lunches, office meetings, boring night clubs, they even stay in the homes of their contacts, whose first names they use slightly anxiously. Deep down they are romantics, travellers, hopers; they know it's not a bit of good, really, trying to find a common language with the factory stay-at-homes, still less the Government. They write mournful letters, knowing no one is listening, to *The Times*, complaining about not being backed up.

You would have to *be* an export manager to get the point of this, which was in the Board of Trade Export Services Bulletin (and who knows about it if they don't?):—

THAILAND

ANTIMONY (Ref ESB/33593/64). The following is the full text of an announcement concerning the above requirements:
AMPHUR WANG-NUA POLICE STATION (Lampang Province). Tender for the purchase of 7,004 Kgs. Antimony. Tenders to be submitted on 15 December at 10 a.m.

Gregory Lequesne, a handsome, greying man, is sipping a Tom Collins among a laughing group on the veranda of the best hotel in Singapore, where he is breaking a journey home from Australia. He frowns at the cable from British Antimony. Since his elder brother, Morton Lequesne, died, soon after B.A. took over Lequesne Bros, an old family antimony firm founded by their Huguenot ancestor (Jacques Lequesne, settled in Soho, friend of printers), he has felt himself to be on sufferance.

'What the hell *is* antimony, Greg?' asks Jim Travers. 'Why don't you chuck it and settle down with me and Mr Wong here?'

'It suits you, Meestair Lequesne,' says a faultless Eurasian beauty. 'Antimoney, yes? I theenk you are not caring about money.'

'I care for *you*, Raka,' says Lequesne. 'Actually it's dreary-looking stuff, but it seems to be in everything. With lead and tin in type metal, with zinc and tin in Britannia metal, whatever that is, with copper and tin and *bismuth* in pewter. There'th no bithmuth like antimony bithmuth.'

All the same, the old excitement stirs. Somehow he had missed Thailand up to now. Seven thousand and four kilograms, that's more than seven *tons* of antimony. He resolves to go himself, not merely submit a tender, if only to annoy that bounder Maxwell, who has taken over as M.D. An old B.A. man, naturally.

Amphur Wang-Nua turns out to be a clearing in charming, hilly, forested country. A smiling man in a uniform, with a shining Sam Browne, comes out from the rural, wooden-built police station as Lequesne dismounts from his horse. 'Ah, the so-welcome Englishman! I am Inspector Pramh Panhang. I am glad to tell you the Germans and Japanese merely posted their tenders. But you have come yourself to us. The contract is yours. But first we will entertain you.'

At the alfresco lunch for marvellous spicy foods and heady drinks ('you will like this, Mr Lequesne. It is distilled from teak bark. It is a little like your *Vieille Cure*'), the police band plays *clong* music and maidens perform graceful dances. 'What's that pile of grey things, Pramh?' asks Lequesne.

'Oh, that is our antimony. Very good. You will like it.'

'But I thought—'

'That you were going to sell *us* antimony. No, look, tender is for *purchase* of antimony. My policemen make it. They have much spare time. There is no crime in Amphur Wang-Nua. Not' (a slight smile) 'since I came here.'

Lequesne looks round at the pastoral scene. 'But—the plant, the equipment? You surely have to roast the sulphide in a reverberatory furnace—'

'We have our own methods, Mr Lequesne. So you do not wish to buy? It is sad. But maybe you stay here, sell *our* antimony. . . .'

ℭ The not Impossible Shee
(with a bow to Crashaw)

Who shee be,
That not impossible shee
That shall command my heart and mee?
Shee'll not be found
In Fashion's Forcing-ground,
Straighte, where a maiden should bee round.
Shee hath a Waiste
Fit to be embrac'd;
Above, below, more amply grac'd.
This model shee
Will not a Model be
Of Vogue-*like Angularitie*
She will not stare
With cold and unsex'd Glare
At cam'ras, as who'ld say Just dare!
I'll not indite
Lines to that chilly Sight
The hollow-ey'd Hermaphrodite.
Her Tresses' Hue
Is matched by Eyebrows true,
Proving no Dyes have made it new.
Nor are those Tresses
Expensive, piled successes
Which Rain converts to soggy Messes.
Her Legges enable
Minis to cloathe a Fable—
Not a mere Jacobean Table
Or, if her Knees
(I care not) be like Trees

Shee hath the Sense to cover these.
Her Voyce is clear
But softe and low to hear
(An excellent Thinge, as said King Lear)
But shee's not dumb
At Parties sitting mum,
Making each Talker feel a bumme;
I'd find unsuitable
A shee who, all inscrutable,
Answer'd with Silence irrefutable.
By Humour and Wit
Her sparkling Eye is lit,
Both Love and Laughter kindling it.
I doubte if shee
An honours graduate bee
But if shee is, 'tis hard to see
(And most of all
The thought doth mee appal
Of Life with one that writes withal;
I'ld like to be
In her good Bookes—not see
In Novells by her, nasty mee).
Let no dull Foole
Think here I make a Rule
To keepe all Beauties out of Schoole
Nor learned shees
With very good degrees
Hearing this, be ill at Ease
And, with a tremble,
All their Braines dissemble
And unletter'd shees resemble;
Let none turn pale
For such shees cannot fail
To win an honours graduate male.

I just take Leave
To say I don't believe
In Learning worn upon the Sleave
(Besides, like Paines
In Necke are shees with Braines
Deeming Children Drags and Drains).
Though shee be letter'd
This qualitie is better'd
In Her by whom my heart is fetter'd,
Better'd by Heart
And all Love knows of Art:
Who be *shee then? Ah! Back to start.*

When the Wurlitzer Had to Stop

✦✦✦

> 'Detectives boarded the Shaw Savill liner *Northern Star* when she docked at Southampton yesterday. They will try to discover who wrecked the cinema organ and a double bass when the ship was in Panama'—*Daily Mail.*

GOOD LORD, I thought the Purser *knew* about the Fairfax-Bensons! I mean, if he didn't, everyone else on the ship did. It's odd in a way, but I suppose I was indirectly responsible for the whole thing. We were doing a round at Wentworth one lovely sunny weekday before the Board Meeting of Peabody Marine; both of us due to retire in rotation.

'Look, F.B.,' I said, 'why don't we skip re-election this year? Take a sabbatical. Cruise, perhaps. We've pulled P.M. out of the red.'

'Thanks to the Butibote,' he grunted. I was on the technical side, I'd designed this mass-produced cruiser for the affluent society. Selling like hot cakes.

'Oh, come, old man,' I riposted, 'who arranged the finance?' (He came to us from the insurance world; lot of City contacts.) 'Bring Dolly, and we'll stave off executive's thrombosis, the three of us.' I'm a bachelor, knocked about the world a bit, known a few women; and although Dolly Fairfax-Benson is a damned handsome woman I assure you there was no ulterior motive in my suggestion. I'd been a regular guest at Coathangers, their place near Leatherhead, for years.

Extraordinary effect a sea voyage and warmer climate has on a woman. They'd always been a devoted pair, no troubles in their marriage as far as I know, but do you know, we hadn't been out of Southampton a day before something got into Dolly. Of course she'd got herself a whole new rig-out for the trip, bell-bottom trousers, things like that. I gather they're the fashion again now; but by George, it took me back to the 'thirties, when they were called beach pyjamas, gals used to wear them with those floppy hats.

Odd thing was, it took Dolly back to the 'thirties too. Fluffed her hair out in big Marcel waves and all that, and kept asking the bandleader at the ship's dances for old Cole Porter numbers and things from Ginger Rogers films. And one couldn't help noticing she danced a great deal with a passenger called Jago—*Rodney* Jago, if you please. Our kind of age, but one of those tans that make you think he has some lamp at home, greying temples, face like old baby, big flashy smile. Wore blazer, white trousers, choke scarf all the time. Didn't care for him myself, and naturally I could see F.B. cared even less. Out of his depth, too, years since he'd tried to sparkle.

This Jago sparkled like hell, all the time, and Dolly lapped it up. One gala night the four of us were sitting at the bar, F.B. staring glumly into his drink, when suddenly it came to me.

'Rodney Jago!' I said. 'The crooning organist of the Granada Leicester Square. Broadcast every week on the National Programme.'

I could have kicked myself. Dolly's eyes lit up. 'Rod, of *course*!' she said. 'I knew there was something familiar. I was a terrific fan, I thought you were better than Reginald Foort. I shall tell the Captain. You must play at the ship's concert!'

'But I'm out of practice, Doll,' said Jago (I saw old

F.B. stiffen at the familiarity). 'I'm what every young idol aims to be—a middle-aged agent. That's where the money is, and it's easier; you don't have to do it yourself!' But it was too late. Dolly told the Captain, and it was all over the ship, people queueing up for his autographs (they were *all* our kind of age). And would you believe it, there was an organ in the ship's cinema, it went blue and pink and had temple gongs and thunderstorms and crying baby noises on it, and went up and down. Just like the old days. Hadn't been used since the war.

'Where the hell does it go down to?' said F.B. 'The engine room?'

'Oh, Don, don't be a jealous spoilsport,' said Dolly. Well, they got this thing going, and one had to admit this Jago knew his stuff. So popular, they couldn't all get in, he was giving three shows a day. The women were all over him, but Dolly was queen. She enjoyed that.

Well, there was an odd twist to the story. When we docked at Panama Dolly went off to some night spot with Jago, and I think I was almost as sore about it as old F.B. We stayed on board and got pretty high, and when he said, 'Whyn't we go down there and turn that thing into a Mangle-wurlitzer?' I was right with him. We went down to the ship's cinema (empty, everyone was on shore) and did a real wrecking job. Then we went back to the bar, and who do you suppose was the only other chap there? Jago, looking pretty glum. She'd ditched him for a swarthy type called Gaspar Ruiz, leader of one of those South American bands that wear tight trousers and frilly shirts. He played the string bass and sang. They *all* sang.

She even got them invited on board to do a show.

My word, there was one hell of a row when they came on and found the double bass wrecked. Waving hands, oaths, storming off, gent in white ducks from the local police. All smoothed over, though, and the Fairfax-Bensons re-united. But I thought the Purser knew, about Jago busting the double bass, and everything.

¢ Cigarette Ashmpoo

✦✦

EXTRAORDINARY HOW it always seems to be early-closing day when want more anti-smoke tablets (in second stage of afumia or addiction to non-smoking, desire is not for cigarettes but anti-smoke tablets, made from lobelias, goodness knows how they found that out, maybe desperate gardener out of cigarettes stuffed dried lobelias in old pipe, was miraculously cured? It is *third* stage when desire for smoke returns, cf. old joke, man offered cigarette, says No thanks, I haven't smoked for 15 years, bursts into tears).

With mad clarity and detachment see whole condition of afumiac* as living in endless, cosmic early-closing day. All joys of life—taste of food, beauty of trees, girls, paintings, whorled ears of babies, sound of music, all that I-have-been-so-great-a-lover stuff, as well as sense of own body, marvellous bones, breath (*hnn,* ha, *hnnn* haagh)—perceived as never before, but all somehow behind tall glass windows in long avenue, nobody about, ghostly silence (non-smoker only man in world) on cold-warm dampish Spring day, faintly hungry feeling.

But ha, have still got two anti-smoke tablets; unfortunately they coated in unique paste made of coal ash and dog shampee (typical typewriter word invented during afumia, I mean of course shapmoo). Nerveless fingers fumbled smart, well-styled, ultra-light

* Note to purists. OK, so it's a hybrid word, the Greek for 'smoke' is kapnos. But be honest, *acapniac* sounds like a man who does sex murders in parks, doesn't it?

plastic pot containing tablets and dropped remaining two into coal ash in hearth last week. Later couldn't find anywhere to put dog hasmpoo except mantelpiece. Room seems filled up with many separate things—old broken cameras (where *from*?), wire things, pieces of worthless simpering figurines which will never be mended. Just about space on mantelpiece for dog pashmoo, what with little dictionaries; candle; deliquescent rock salt figure from salt mine which once went down in Poland; old filigree car with no wheels; clock on which, when was gay, carefree smoker in unrecognizable past (but ha, not so healthy, didn't breathe hnn, haagh *then*), stuck headline cut out from city page, COMPULSORY WINDING-UP; cup won for cross-country in Bangalore in 1944 . . .

Damn, knocked dog shmapoo over, it got no stopper, splash right on tablet buried in ash. Ha, will come to terms with mad dreams of Bangalore, Poland, etc.; will act, will *do,* will drive eight miles (hnn, haagh, hnn, HAAGH) to nearest place where it not early-closing, buy more tablets.

Chemist there not got usual kind, which are sort of little black sweets; he only got other kind like pills (white; only colour lobelia pills don't seem to be is blue). With them comes tremendous leaflet, *The University Plan to Help you Stop Smoking* (*. . . research in laboratories of one of America's leading universities . . .*).

Your first day will be your hardest, says leaflet (nonsense, this my hardest day so far, I make it the 47th). *You CAN stop, you know. Remember, you go all night without smoking when you are asleep . . . throw or give away all cigarettes, cigars, or pipe tobacco. Tell your family and friends that you have given up smoking. Feel sorry for them because they are unable . . . to wean themselves from the tobacco habit . . . as the days go by, look your old enemy in the eye. Light the other fellow's cigarette—and feel sorry for him* . . . (If merely cutting down) *change the pocket where you ordinarily carry your cigarettes, cigars, pipe or snuff* . . . (*Note: men can change pockets, but for women who carry cigarettes in their purse, we recommend . . . etc.*).

God bless soul, what kind of man they think give up smoking? What exhibitionist! He call meeting of family and friends, perhaps even hire hall if he got enough of them. I've called you all here because I'm giving up smoking; here's 200 Players for *you,* my old meerschaum for *you,* hubble-bubble for *you* . . . like reading of will (can't smoke when you're *dead* either, why they not put that in leaflet?). Or perhaps all gather by river bank, mad formal act, the Throwing Away of the Pipes.

And how awful to meet such man on the 47th day; you would unconsciously get out cigarette and he would say No, let me, fumble frantically in pocket for matches (no, of course, not that pocket, he changed it, it just got peppermints, lozenges, gum, worry-pebble and lobelia pills in there now), look straight in your eye, mad intense look, he say, I feel sorry for you my poor fellow, you missing all that's fine and true; like Victorian evangelist reclaiming sot. Then he go home to unimaginable family all puffing away and feel sorry for *them,* e.g., his wife, as well he might if she got snuff, etc., in her *purse*. . . .

Go home self and wash ash, haspoom, off little black sweet. On to 48th and probably last day. Everyone else can be sorry for my family; family can be sorry for *me*.

ℭ Lines Written in Despondency in Trafalgar Square

(On the proposal to impose a 20p admission charge for museums and art galleries)

◆◆◆

Through portico-pillars, up stately stone steps
ascending,
Harmless-for-once humanity smiles,
Admiring, inspired, untiring at vistas unending
Of modes and madonnas, of statues and styles,
Of dreams and dimensions, angelical lineaments
captured,
Severe Sienese with a stiffness of stuff,
Gabriel-gaudium, wonder of wings to a virgin
enraptured,
Velvet or vestment, a veil or a ruff
Framing ferocious or foxified, water-eyed fellows,
Eyes of the miser, the loser, the proud,
Lances and lines of perspective-exultant Uccellos,
Riot and ruin and castle and crowd,
Figures in forecourts, beyond them a marvel inviting,
Feathery trees on pink stone hills
In landscapes to linger and long for, delighting,
Easing the eye from earth and its ills;
Later, a largesse of light all dappled and stippled,
Fractured and hatched in a noon of France,
Lines in their loveliness rounded and ravelled and
rippled,
Credo-created, a cosmos in dance:

Museums, so magic and marvellous, making us wonder
Daily in dalliance with real and ideal,

What is this mumble and marching, this threat as of
thunder?
Who dares to say *you shall not feel*
Unless you pay?
—O God, a dreadful army comes
Of foppish hardhats, po-faced bowlered bums
Whose mealy minds, whose souls of dust and ash
Chafe for the chance of turning art to cash.

¢ 3 O'Clock and All's Deafening

3 A.M. Sounding through a confused dream about the end of the world, which everyone is expecting utterly without emotion, as though it were a kind of grey Bank Holiday with the whole human race, carrying shabby suitcases, waiting stolidly on Platform 14 for the train to infinity, is a piercing reedy note.

I am at a concert; Dr Mary Stocks comes in and touches my elbow, saying: 'Come on, it's the end of the world, what are you doing in here?' and several of us push out through the orchestra, which is playing marvellous music, although this one persistent note, louder and louder, suggests they are tuning up as well. They seem to be simultaneously in the Albert Hall and in some big station among the trains. We want to be outside, presumably Kensington Gardens, for the end of the world. The note gets more intense.

Suddenly I wake, in—a cupboard? Part of an old library? A shoe shop? Limbo? 1937? The body of someone I don't know? Ah, yes, of course this tall, thin room full of shoes and cream wood is the spare room of Harblow's flat. I am staying the night in London, I know who I am, and it's 1969. The piercing note, which is still going on, is the horn of a diesel train which has stuck.

Trains have been rattling in and out of my dreams since I went to bed. Surely it wasn't like this when *I* lived in London? Then, it seemed to be either one occasional train panting up from Euston with lead ingots and letters for Scotland engraved on stone, or (since words arrange themselves like this at 3 a.m.) the recapitulating clatter-clink of coupled coal-trucks doubly rebounding and banging about, to culminate in the squeaky wrench and steam-shriek of shunting.

But now, the shunting doubtless sophisticated and silent with new continuous brakes, the sound seems to be one of the very light trains bucketing *round* London all night, perhaps along those mysterious lines which one crosses at right-angles two or three miles outside any London terminus; one never sees a train on them, but the rails disappearing into black brick cuttings are bright with use.

It is not the purposeful, matter-of-fact sound of day trains, first stop Harrow or Croydon. There is something random and unscheduled about this wild speed, as though some giant boy, in the Albert Hall perhaps, were switching them on and off. Or could they be having nightly railway sports, a relay race round London, with slick baton-changing at Clapham and Neasden? Whatever they're doing, the horn has stuck.

Perhaps it is a driving lesson, at the only time when learners can use uncluttered tracks. Some young trainee, or possibly an older man being transferred from steam, has done an irreversible thing to the horn button, with results a hundred times worse than it is in a car.

The frightful, remorseless noise blazes out over London as the instructor, named Parsons, wrenches at a locked panel over which he is enraged to see a new sign reading ENGINEERS ONLY. KEYS WITH D.S. Mouthing words which it is as well his companion, a youth called Driver Endicott, cannot hear, he scribbles a note *Phone 3 Shed for key*.

Endicott opens the cab door, admitting a blast of even more terrible sound (for a new circuit has been made which causes the sound to grow indefinitely until the horn melts), clambers down and stumbles off up the tracks.

He is away for ages. Panting into a signal box half a mile off he telephones No. 3 Shed, but the voice at the other end says, 'I can't let you have a key without an S.23. Where's Mr Parsons, then?'

Parsons, at the centre of an inferno of sound, is going mad. He is not quite sure where the horn is on this particular model, and he is jabbing savagely through a louvre with a crowbar when Driver Endicott returns and writes, in the weak light of the headlamp (for the horn is now taking nearly all the electricity), *They want an S.23.*

Parsons flings the crowbar down in a rage. It bounces on the rail and hurts his knee. He seizes the paper from Endicott and scrawls * * * *them, we'll reverse to Depot.* With a dreadful belching roar of full power, audible for a moment even above the demoniacal hooting, he drives furiously backwards along an obscure line to Nine Elms, or Stratford, which the giant boy has previously removed to the end of Harblow's road.

Meanwhile in the nearer houses glass ornaments and little metal boxes dance and vibrate, curtains made of some synthetic fibres disintegrate, flies and mice drop dead. In the strange undark London night, now illuminated with a blaze of all-covering sound as though by an air-raid flare, families with towels tied round their heads come into kitchens and start numbly eating cornflakes, others make tents of blankets and old overcoats under which they bawl down the telephone at police, fire brigades, Euston Sleepers, the B.B.C. Emergency vans full of men in dyed battledress with coils of rope, hatchets, ear-muffs, axes, spades, pummers, poles, armoured torches, nets, special pliers, wrenches, tarpaulins, sandbags, insulated gloves, hosepipes, wire and rubber hammers, screech up cul-de-sac streets ending at railway lines, and reverse furiously as they search fruitlessly for the centre of the pandemonium.

At last it stops. By the watch in my head it has gone on for 50 minutes. I drift back to the Albert Hall, where Dr Stocks is now conducting. In the morning Harblow says he heard nothing.

But I'm perfectly certain I didn't dream *all* of it.

All Called Weedle

THE THING one can never be sure about with cats is whether they are miles ahead of dogs, having tried this communication with men thousands of years ago ('the hell with it,' they said to themselves, in non-words, 'cats will never be able to talk, and anyway there's no such thing as a real concept; let's just *be*, moving softly like furry spirits, sometimes yowling godless, atonal music to chaos and old night, sometimes killing with casual clockwork efficiency, sometimes purring with mindless pleasure')—or are they miles behind, purely automatic, simply like very large ants, millions of years behind the dog whose eyes say *thou, thou*?

Martin Buber, in *I and Thou,* says, 'an animal's eyes have the power to speak a great language . . . the stammering of nature at the first touch of spirit, before it yields to spirit's cosmic venture that we call man . . . (questioned me) "is it possible that you think of me? Do I concern you? Do I exist in your sight?" . . . the animal's glance, speech of disquietude, rose in its greatness—and set at once . . . the almost unnoticeable sunrise and sunset of the spirit.'

But he says this of his *cat.* It must have been different from ours. Now our dog, a spaniel called Barker, worries constantly about whether he exists, he terribly wants to be this actual man called Vernon Peters, or Bellamy Norton, with a kind, stupid face, who smokes a pipe and models great chunky cardigans in knitting books. But the cats don't give a damn, unless it's to try and make us wonder whether *we* exist.

We seem to have three; Elliot the Cat-Mother, Thomas

Tomkins, the Crown Prince (unmarried, weird hobbies), and the Next Cat, called Gallant Captain Dreadful (six weeks old, been eating mice for two of them). We got him as a replacement for Elliot who is 11 and should be dead and is not in the least grateful to us for not having the heart to take the vet's advice and bring this about.

There's nothing wrong with her (she eats like a horse) except that she won't go out, *at all*, and there's always some corner, inaccessible to mops, where we forget to put pepper (and in any case, I don't believe the pepper puts her off, I believe she has trained herself to like pepper and eats it all up). She has hated us, and the entire cosmos, since *she* was six weeks old.

None of them seems to me to think anything about anything, unless it is Captain Dreadful, who may well think he is a child's hat from the way they lug him about on their heads. These cats make it crystal clear that their names, human messages sent out by us, have nothing to do with them really—and I don't believe, with T. S. Eliot (one L), that they have secret names known only to themselves.

The only name that evokes any response at all is *Weedle*. This word shouted several times in a very high, squeaky voice at night, when we are opening their tins, brings Captain Dreadful skipping from inside the piano (only refuge from children), Tomkins clumping downstairs from his blanket-unweaving, and Elliot, in her longest move of the day, growling down from the shelf where she sits emitting occasional peppery belches. Maybe all cats think they are called Weedle Weedle.

This impression that they are sitting about waiting for some non-human Pirandello to create the rest of their character and give them identity is heightened by the fact that we live in the country. In London, cats catch mice, they at least have a functional existence. But our house faces mice the way Hong Kong faces the Communists of China.

If all the mice in our garden, and the bit of land beyond it called The Gritches, let alone the surrounding fields, were to walk past a single point, the procession would never end; and the cats know this. Besides, they prefer rabbits and partridges and birds and the stuff in those tins. They solve the menacing problem of the gritchmice by simply not thinking about it.

One of the gritchmice came to live under our bedroom floor. There is something terribly insolent about a mouse sneezing, which he did constantly. Then came a sound like tiny hammering, as though he was fixing up a flat. We felt we had better do something before they all came in to this rehousing scheme. We lifted up a board and brought up Elliot, who promptly lay down in front of the electric fire, as if to say, 'At last! The blighters realize I'm cold.'

We jerked a tuft of paper on a string along the groove to give Captain Dreadful the idea, but he simply wanted to go on playing with that. We couldn't find Tomkins, so we shouted *Weedle weedle,* at which he instantly appeared, gave us a look of infinite disgust when he saw there was nothing to eat, and went out again.

The only one who really tried was Barker. He put his foot through the plaster.

¢ Beldame Elliot: Great Anti-pet

(A *Times* obituary)

THE DEATH of Beldame Elliot, for many years senior cat in the Jennings household, has severed an interesting link with the early days of that organization. She joined as a young kitten in the year of its foundation, and her career covered the period of remarkable expansion which began almost immediately.

That this expansion reflected a policy of which she deeply disapproved cannot be doubted, for it was not in her nature to dissemble. In fact it would have been revealed to those close to her that she had only joined under the assumption that she was to be the sole recipient of all dividends of love, food and comfort—had anyone been able to get close to her; but as a colleague once jokingly remarked, all relationships with Elliot started from scratch and ended with scratch.

With unshakeable strength of character she stayed on after the crisis in her career when it became clear that the expansion policy had won the day. In the event, her unique, superbly professional talent for hatred, her integrity as a small bristling bundle of total dislike for all the other cats, dogs and children who went about their business in the larger premises acquired in 1956, proved to be an essential counter-ingredient, like the dash of lemon-juice in a sweet sauce. Certainly, few who made her acquaintance in her later years, which she spent mostly growling on a shelf (she retired from active life with a small Uncivil List pension some years ago) could have realized with what remarkable success she totally concealed her delightful sense of humour; she had been an accomplished purrer in early youth, but gave it up late in 1952, the year of the organization's first child.

Hellcat Hateface Elliot was born in June, 1952, the twenty-eighth daughter of Sappho Spitfire Gregory and (probably) the Hampstead Cemetery Cat, a colourful character who later became the first of her own several husbands. There was eastern blood on her mother's side, and the exquisite grace with which she could save anyone the embarrassment of showing affection—arching her back, glaring, walking away from those who foolishly attempted to stroke her—could well have been owed to some delicately formalized old code of hatred. Yet, as the V-shaped cut on one of her ears proclaimed, she never shrank from the more direct hammer-and-tongs set-to of our western tradition. She combined the two cultures in an amalgam of her own.

Her early upbringing was along conventional lines, and from it none could have foreseen that the playful kitten who came to the small London house, in those far-off days when people still bought fish for their cats, would be a pioneer of the Anti-pet revolution. For as certainly as Robbe-Grillet and Sarraute suggest the Anti-novel or Jimmy Porter the Anti-hero, Elliot *was* the Anti-pet.

Her achievement was the more remarkable in that it sprang from a background with no revolutionary tradition of cruelty to cats. As she herself acknowledged in fastidiously reacting from it, conventional love was all that the organization could offer her, at any rate in its non-cat personnel. (Some critics, however, commenting on the Anti-pet movement have noticed that the advent of Barker, the most un-catlike and loving of all dogs, a spaniel, was the final phase in the expansion policy, the final term in the series cats-children-dog; and they have suggested that the very intensity of his love and his desire for love may, *per contra,* have stimulated Elliot to perfect her extraordinary technique of withdrawal.

Will her work live? The two surviving cat members of the organization, Thomas Tomkins and Captain Dreadful, are still in their formative years. The former, a rabbit-eater by profession, and something of a free-lance (he visits for long periods any other organization that will give him food) is precluded by occupational somnolence from expressing any attitude at all, whether of hate or love. The latter seems quite ready to hate anyone engaged in eating while he is (or is not), but observers have agreed that this is more greed than hate; and he still purrs. Neither, therefore, is an Anti-pet in the true Elliot sense, and it remains to be seen whether this movement will become a living tradition or, like so many in the past, simply a dead end, the flowering of one rogue personality.

She leaves 33 children, apart from several who predeceased her. (One grandson, William Byrd, died of a mysterious illness, and it was alleged in some quarters that she had put a spell on him; but the case was not pursued.)

T.T. writes: In your excellent obituary of my dear old enemy Elliot, I noticed there was no mention of her prowess in the hunting field. Perhaps I may be allowed to qualify the suggestion that the 1956 move from London was entirely unwelcome to her by recalling her delight in the abundant sport afforded by the county of my forebears.

Though she was a somewhat gruff companion on our expeditions, her sheer professionalism made her a joy to watch. She killed for the pure joy of the thing and never seemed to eat her prey, merely biting off its head and generously leaving the meat to others like myself. She will be sadly missed by hunters and *bons-viveurs*.

⊄ Lumbered

FOR YEARS now I have been thinking comfortably that there is an enormous gap between all normal households and the ones you see in illustrated features. You know the kind of thing. 'Architect John S. and his Swedish-born wife in their converted oast-house. It's a basic, primitive shape for living, says John, like a wigwam or tepee. They ripped out all floors to make one huge, conical space. Free-floating bedrooms are connected by spidery balconies. Children are safe below in free play area.' The picture shows one child with three building blocks on a spotless floor.

Or: 'Actress Successa Pinhead is completely re-decorating her Belgravia flat now she's back from the triumphant Russian tour of the London smash lesbian comedy *The Passionate Spinsters* (specially asked for by the Russians; "they're deeply interested in our way of life," says Successa). Cool muslin swags, unpainted zinc balloons, tall unsized canvas moveable walls mean the eating area can be expanded when Successa and husband Joe Joe Jones, the abstract carpenter, give cook-ins for theatrical friends.' The picture to this is a black settee, costing £315 (and I haven't made *that* up), a centre brazier under a kind of copper *baldacchino,* a shelf with four books and 218 LP's in a neat row.

Even when the people and houses represented are nearer the kind one actually knows ('warm reds, browns and blacks give the basic Streatham ground floor a new luxury. When Colin comes home from the Prudential ...') these interiors all have something that isolates them.

And that something is *tidiness.*

Even if these people don't have children, where the hell are their slippers? Where are their old camera cases, pipes, faded canvas bags, japanned boxes with no lids, souvenirs of the Eiffel Tower, dropped flower petals, mugs containing tubes of glue that have burst at the side and now adhere to halves of scissors, buttons, nuts, pins and watch-keys? (Nobody in our house has a keyed watch, but we have watch-keys.) Where are their not-quite-worn-out espadrilles, sewing machines, hats, music, empty tonic bottles, towels, cake-tins with old soggy biscuits inside, alarm clocks not thrown away because they will still go when face downwards?

Above all, where's the *paper,* the piles and sheaves of letters and folders and bills and holiday guides and calendars and leaflets, on tables, shelves, window-sills, stuffed behind clocks? Where are the dreadful sliding heaps of old magazines?

And if they do have children, where are the drawings on the wallpaper (all my children have taken the expression 'drawing-room' at its face value)? Where are the hard knots in the carpet pile caused by Airfix glue? Where (for three or more children) the 13 odd Wellington boots ...

Anyone who leads a normal life could go on endlessly with such a list, for surely normal life *is* untidy. I'm not making a virtue of this, nor has it anything much to do with litter and mess at picnic sites. It's perfectly easy for any normal family to be tidy at a picnic, however messy they are at home, because a picnic is, in fact, one of the few occasions when a family is doing one organized thing all together—a clear-cut, communal enterprise with a definite beginning and end, requiring conscious quasi-military planning. It's one thing to leave a field tidy when everyone is about to perform the willed act of getting into the car. It's quite another to keep a house tidy where one activity endlessly flows into another. The phone rings while something is being mended, then it's time for supper, a dog, cat or child pulls out all the wool, a dictionary is brought down to the kitchen where someone is doing homework because someone else is practising the piano (or should be—why has it gone quiet in there?) in the room where the homework should have been done an hour ago, *all* the children step on the edge of the dog's dinner plate and spill it, letters meant to be answered quickly are put in some special place, in—*surely* I put it under that jug . . .

A house in which any kind of real life is lived will be like that. I've mentioned children because we have them, but they aren't really necessary for the creation of that untidiness which it is so cheering for us normal, non-magazine-feature people to find in another house; the special dimension of mess added by children has to do with their endless spilling and knocking over things, from their own mugs or pots to those confounded won't-stand-up Rice Krispie packets. They grow out of that (one hopes), but the tendency to cover every flat surface with odd *things,* that don't fit into any category and don't really belong in any imaginable cupboard is something that ought to go right on into any adult life.

I've seen it in plenty of comfortable bachelor and spinster households too; a kitchen with unsmart dressers, tottering piles of bent saucepans, jars full of half-fermented rhubarb wine, drawers crammed with old Christmas cards, skewers, tangled string, tortoise-shell things, yellowing recipes, a round boxwood box with some Edwardian menthol in it, a forgotten camera. Or a music room smelling powerfully of cats, containing half a dozen chairs but never ready for a chance visitor without the removal of a cat, or seven books, or a tray with five cocoa cups dating from last Tuesday. There may be only one occupant of such a house, but you can deduce happiness, absorption, a constant moving from one interest to another like a dog following its nose on a joyous walk. You don't need children for that kind of comfortable mess—although it is to this kind of interior that our children seem to be made most welcome.

Until very recently I thought I knew more households like this than I did neat, smile-please uncluttered ones. Suddenly this is not so. It's not that all our cheerfully untidy friends have just gone away or died (dammit, I'm only 50), but suddenly they are in a minority. Naturally, since more and more people are living in estates that have communal tidy lawns and two horizontal white planks all round instead of untidy hedges, we find ourselves in houses where they *start off* tidy; from the moment they're married they have a complete stock of everything all new, all neat (how on earth do they do it, we haven't got a sideboard in the dining room *yet*, and we've been married 16 years?). They have this tidy family, of 2.3 children, and these children are neat, too.

Well, one expects that; but it's unsettling when one of our trusted, known-for-years untidy households gets a face-lift; suddenly there are no more dark corners, there's a lot more glass, whiteness, straight lines, space, papers are organized in enormous bulldog clips or even funny giant clothes pegs inscribed BIG DEAL, hanging on a neat hardboard panel. And of course there's a lot of natural wood. It's like going into Coventry Cathedral after—well, after the *old* Coventry Cathedral.

I think perhaps the turning point was the Clean Air Act. The open fireplace, now everywhere replaced by various kinds of discreet louvre, was a survival from the pre-machine age—the age of unique, separate, unstandardized things. Once the open fire went the standardizing pressure of the machine, which had been gathering for generations, quickly caused this complete change in people's ideas of what a domestic interior should look like; clean, bright, uncluttered, and above all tidy.

The machine had at last achieved inside our houses what it had long since achieved outside. The car, for instance, has been getting tidier all the time. Once the saloon (as we called it) was dearer than the tourer (as we called it) simply because there was more metal in it. Now the convertible is dearer because it's *untidier,* fussier to make than the saloon which can be clonked out of a giant press. The diesel is tidier than the steam train. All the ice cream in England tastes exactly the same, from Wallsend to Cornwall, and I'm sure it's a tidier system. At fairgrounds fluorescent lighting (from tidy diesel generators, not great thudding steam engines) is tidier than the old rows of bulbs—and you never see a really untidy naphtha flare at all. Washing-machines are tidier than mangles and dolly-tubs, a VC 10 is tidier than an Imperial Airways flying-boat (with those wicker chairs and aspidistras), electric razors are tidier than all that lather (thank God. This isn't a list of complaints, merely a statement of fact).

But we still find that every flat surface in our house is covered by old *Listeners,** the lids of jigsaw puzzles, socks, exercise books, important letters (or at any rate letters that were important in February 1958), carpet

* And I mean old, before it became the *Sociology Times.*

samples, record sleeves containing two or no records, even old bread and cheese.

I know, roughly, where everything is, I hope. But before it actually becomes a legal offence for one's domestic interior not to look as new, neat and universal as everyone else's, let me suggest a slight alteration to the famous line of Marvell's . . .

'The grave's a fine and *tidy* place.'

¢ The Ohm Fires

THERE IS something faintly disturbing about electricity in the country. In London you feel that the cables go on past the house to supply great factories thudding, clanking and bomping away making pieces of ships or printing the labels for tins of tomatoes; to long Government corridors smelling of green paint; to halls full of people shouting or singing or gripped by a thrilling communal silence; to hospitals, schools, churches even —the whole complex of civilization.

But in our house there is a terminus feeling, there's nowhere else for the electricity to go after us, there's nothing behind the house but an untidy parcel of land littered with sodden charred newspaper blown out from under the grating over which children have tried to boil, or at least smoke, a mess of carrots, bread, raisins and seashells.

The electricity comes across murky fields, often cut off by unexplained rural hazards (bees drinking the oil in the transformers? Flying cows incinerated on the pylons? Maintenance men turned into toads? Who knows?). Men in white coats in the power stations look down the cables at us to see if we are making the most of it, they keep sending us leaflets about strange heaters that mysteriously *save* electricity.

All houses are, with their warm human life inside, the nearest that matter ever gets to spirit except for the actual flesh of man, and this dimly moves them to twist the natural tendency of matter to fall apart, drag down, sleep for a million years, become small and nothing, into their own parody of the Life Force, which I can only call Life Decay. When they go damp, develop strange rots, thrombosis of the pipes, become suddenly too small in some rooms, or even lean over so as to bend the floor, houses are dimly calling out for the human activity of repair and renewal, like animals calling out for a soul.

Our house, rightly suspecting that electricity, which is really just matter getting above itself, will ultimately dispense with houses altogether in some Wellsian artificial summer, uses all its powers of Life Decay against it. Men come and rewire us but within a year all overhead lights are again suspended from wires round which curl shreds of a brittle substance that seems of Pompeian antiquity and crumbles at the touch. Switches lose their ability to click and become loose in the wall. The radio gets quieter and quieter and goes *a-a-a-a-a* (only much faster than that) whenever an *aeroplane* comes over (there is also a portable, known as the Burnt Pye, which was either left on a convector heater by a child or got up there itself, so that all the bits flowed into one another, and now it will only *stop* when ribbon is tied round it with a tight bow. Something keeps sizzling to itself in the fuse box.

The men in white coats keep sending us reproachful messages about immersion heaters, but the house keeps gently immersing and smothering the electric fires we already have, remorselessly weakening them until they develop little white-hot spitting globules at the ends of the elements. The guard jumped off one of them in the middle of the night with a frightful twanging noise, when it wasn't even switched on. We have one of those tea-making alarm clocks that will either make tea and sound the alarm without switching the light on, switch the light on and make tea without sounding the alarm, or sound the alarm and switch the light on without making tea, but never all three at once, as it is supposed to.

The plug in the spare bedroom emits a frightful smell of burning bakelite, so when we have visitors we give them our newest electric fire (i.e. the only one that doesn't spit or actually give off cold. I try polishing them but the old ones still do this) and plug it in for them on the landing, since the thick flex easily passes under the door (this is one of the places where the house has leant over)—in itself a proof how much a fire is needed to counteract the draught, let alone satisfy a guest like my friend Harblow, who lives in London and is faintly surprised not to see reindeer when he visits us. He always brings a huge bag which I suspect contains more blankets to reinforce the seven we give him. Last time, he asked for a hook and some string.

'Do you want some worms as well?'

'No, a *screw* hook. Shove it in the floor by the plug, tie the string to the switch, pass it under the hook, you can pull it to switch the fire on in the morning without getting out of bed.' (It was encouraging to hear he didn't have it on all night.) He insisted on rigging up a similar contraption for our own room as well. Other hooks were required to bring the line round corners. (Hooks look extraordinary upside down, on floors. People discovering this house in 500 years' time will say, 'Good heavens, it used to be the other way up.') String broke, wire was too strong and pulled a hook out of the floor. We went to a town nine miles away to buy special strong twine; it had rather got us now, we spent most of Saturday on it. It was only in the morning we remembered that the switches are upside down and pulling the string switched the fires off, except that of course they were off already.

¢ I've Got the Furies in

OUR HOUSE is being singled out by wasps. Or perhaps by one, special wasp. In December. It's very creepy. Other people have wasps in July (and so do we, of course) but I have never met anyone else who, round about the middle of December, hears this low, despondent *hnahhr*-ing noise from behind the bedroom curtain or inside the bedside lamp. If Charon, on a slack day when there were not many souls to be ferried across the Styx, were to sit down under a leafless tree in the gloomy fog and play one intermittent low note on some hellish kind of *cor anglais,* that is what it would sound like: *hnahhr, hnahhr,* or perhaps *hnohhr* . . .

I have never cared for those Aerosol sprays which not only seem to give the little blighters some kind of galloping peritonitis which I would not wish even on to a wasp, but simultaneously suffuse the air with Synthetic Jasmine or Night of Love. It is like using a machine gun, while wearing a dinner jacket, against naked savages. Wasps should be either stared out or engaged in mortal combat.

In any case, wasps are usually too quick to let you read labels and small print; and our pantry is dotted with Aerosol tins of other stuff, like varnish and hair lacquer and, would you believe it, *starch.* If you can squirt starch you can surely squirt anything; there will be Aerosol tins of porridge next. There is something awful about the idea of a starched wasp. And another thing about Aerosol fly-killers is that before the wasps actually die they suddenly whizz about with a lunatic, up-and-down abandon which makes it much harder to get out of their way than it is when they are doing their usual flying, as though they were searching for something and had forgotten what it was.

Why do I think it is only one wasp? Well, for several reasons really. They sort of add up. Even though, several times, I have banged at the curtain, or knocked over the bedside table lamp, lunging with a rolled-up newspaper at wherever the *hnahhr* was coming from, and eventually undoubtedly killed the creature, there is something, a baleful here-I-am-again look, about the next appearance, that worries me. And then it is such a funny size. Big, well-fed looking (my encyclopaedia says they chew 'rotten old posts' in the winter; I have got plenty of those, but this creature in the bedroom is obviously way above the rotten old post line. It is too big for an ordinary stinger and not big enough for a queen). I have come to believe it is the *same* wasp, some kind of immortal, and is trying to stare me out.

You must not think that I have not done the obvious things first. At one time I too made the obvious and simple deduction, as everyone does who gets crowds of wasps upstairs in July (for normally wasps like to cruise six inches above the kitchen floor, where they can come at your ankles from behind), that we had a wasps' nest in the roof.

There are a lot of things that *could* be wasps' nests in our roof, a place of gothic twilight and horror where, as one treads on joists with a dreadful sagging curvature not reflected by any known ceiling underneath, drifting tendrils of God knows what brush one's face as in a funfair Ghost Train. Indeed the splashes and gobbets of plaster, the tumbling spirals of filthy old brown felt and withered newspaper clinging to water-pipes, and the great looming cobwebs, look like the remnants of some hectic devils' dance up there, shrivelled up at cock-crow.

But until I can get a frogman's suit I cannot be quite sure about wasps' nests. I should need a frogman's suit to feel safe anywhere near the eaves, where it would be impossible to back out quickly. You do not catch me creeping up there in ordinary clothes and inserting 'a ball of cotton wool soaked in cyanide at the entrance to the nest', as it says in the encyclopaedia ('the nest may be removed after a few hours'). I have looked at this thing, in the summer, through a plastic telescope belonging to one of my children, and there have never been more wasps there than anywhere else. Both before and after the official council man came (*he* would not go near it, either) there was usually just this one wasp, cruising. The man lit some kind of sober municipal firework, which caused dense yellow smoke to ooze out through the tiles (it looked spectacular from the garden) but when I went to look ('after a few hours'), there It still was. A bit dozy-looking, but still there.

Finally, there is the mythological information in the encyclopaedia. It says: 'Seven species of *Vespidae,* which are social, and the *Eumenes and Odynerus,* which are solitary, predominate among the 290 or so species in Britain.' You see? *Eumenes,* that's what I've got. *Eumenes,* one of the *Eumenides,* or Furies. I've got a Fury.

Why? What have *I* done? The Furies (or *Eumenides,* in the beautiful old Greek legend, formed from the drops of blood when Cronos castrated his father Uranus) are familiar, to anyone who has seen T. S. Eliot's *The Family Reunion,* as a couple of stage hands with luminous eyebrows standing in a window embrasure to scare the hell out of Harry, who pushed his wife off a liner;

and they have bigger ideas than just defiling food. They torment those 'who have committed crimes of perjury, murder, inhospitality, or violation of filial duty.' There are supposed to be three of them: Alecto, Megaera and Tisiphone.

Oh, I say, look here! I have never murdered anyone, and as for inhospitality, why, we gave quite a big party early in December and three lots of Christmas drinks as well. That damned Tisiphone, or whoever it is, can go down and look for itself at all the bottles still waiting to get into the dustbin. (I bet the dustmen don't think we are inhospitable, I bet they think we have got an off-licence, I bet they imagine great Hogarthian breakfasts, the children pouring gin on their cornflakes; I have never seen so many bottles; and they must think we *burn shoes* at these breakfasts too. Bottles and burnt shoes, that is what our bins are full of. And I have not done those other crimes, perjury and that, either.)

But it is no good for that thing to lurk there and go *hnahhr* at me. I intend to stare It out—and that goes for Alecto and Megaera too. I am going to get up into that loft again, when it is really cold, and see if there are any of those social *Vespidae* in that horrible grey-white thing. I will wait till they are numbed by frost, and I will borrow a frogman's uniform somewhere. And if I do find any, there is going to be some real inhospitality and murder. Christmas notwithstanding.

℄ My Scorched-earth Policy

✦✦

As a spectacle, my weed-killing is at its most dramatic at twilight. Sound seems to carry better in the still evening air, and as people draw near they can hear the deep growling roar, or they can guess what I'm doing from the occasional flashes of sulphurous yellow light that show up the house in the gathering dusk—unless they're new to the area, in which case God knows what they think I've got round there at the back. A natural gas strike, perhaps, or the finals of the World Plumbing Competition, a hundred champion plumbers with their roaring blow-torches in the compulsory Wiped Joint Figure; or the gateway to hell. For what I do is burn weeds. I burn them with a contraption that is, essentially, a monster blow-torch, over three feet long and weighing about fifteen pounds. It is called a Flame Wand.

When I first got it the Flame Wand was simply that year's experiment. Every year the gardening shops come out with the season's magic device, which will realize at last the ancient human dream of Making Gardening Easy; strange lawn-edgers with wheels, a canvas thing for sucking up leaves (the picture shows a woman pushing it along with one hand while she touches up her hair with the other). Many of the devices seem aimed at people with lumbago. I recall a curious curved stick with a knife edge with which you were supposed to take a casual swipe at nettles as you passed (as if one *could* be casual about nettles. They're not casual about me, they lean over to sting me). And there was an implement described by its makers as a Swoe. Some of these things survive and are taken into the repertory, others rust in the shed after the first experiment and are never heard of again.

But I've had the Flame Wand for three years now. Never mind about the garden, it's done *me* a lot of good. I was beginning to feel I'd lost out to weeds. I have read that there are only two genuine primeval forests in England. Well, there is only one primeval weed-thicket, and I've got it. Little low bushes, briars, and stunted, throttled trees—weed-*trees,* I have—struggle through growths of a richness and complexity that would bring specialists from all over the world, if they could find a way to get in. It surrounds my garden on three sides, it sends long yellow cable-like roots underground.

I don't only have the usual thistles and shepherd's purse and groundsel and ground elder (the latter smugly intertwined with the roots of roses and peonies, smirking there, knowing I can't destroy it without destroying them). I have mediaeval, *druid* weeds long since banished from the rest of the country by the Cistercian monks who taught Europe farming and pushed back the frontiers of the wilderness: long-vanished, evil things like Fogwort, Devil's Eyeball, Tinsy, Thrust, Old Man's Trousers, Worritweed, Pox, Death-gripe, Jack o' Bedlam, Common Flannel, Creeping Judas, Hellsbane, Maid's Madness, Hangover, Blasphemy, Arson, Beelzebub's Fork, Malice, and Frumpity.

These things have been coming up for thousands of years, dying after each summer and releasing another uncountable number of seeds. I have dug the ground. I have bought a machine with a 2½ h.p. motor and great metal blades that chomp up the soil, I have scattered deadly chemicals. But ten days after I have achieved a perfect flat brown expanse of pure soil, that uniform, evil green beard has been started up all over again (and Shakespeare was wrong, by the way, to say that lilies that fester smell far worse than weeds. Even while they're alive these weeds smell quite as bad as any old festering lily). It's not machines I want, it's an exorcist.

Or so I thought until I got the Flame Wand (good name, come to think of it: there is a suggestion of exorcism and magic about the word *wand*). Ha, things are different now.

I am out most nights with it. I've got the damnedest, flattest, brownest, neatest vegetable bed you ever saw. After every two or three burnings I chomp it up with my machine, to bring some more seeds to the top. Then I burn *them.* All previous operations like this have left me with more soil that I had to begin with, not to mention all the stuff left by the neolithic armourer and dentist who once shared premises on this very spot. In the past I've had to add to the rubbish-tumulus already five feet high beyond the garden. But now the level is actually going down, I am gradually burning out this vast deposit of weed seeds, getting back to just pure soil.

There is opposition, of course. I turn the mighty flame on to an embryonic creeping buttercup or dandelion, and *the bud opens,* the weed-flower defiantly opens out in a hellish false instant Spring before I fry it. Bats come twinking at me in the gloaming, and once I was attacked by a stag-beetle, like a dreadful little helicopter. That was when I found that the Flame Wand is no use as anti-aircraft defence. The moment you point it upwards it goes out and hot paraffin runs down your sleeve.

But the weeds are going. Last year I found that the green post-ten-days growth contained fewer and fewer weeds. But it also contained more and more of a particularly fine grass, grass such as grew on the innocent earth in the beginning, before the Curse of the Weeds was pronounced.

Could I have made one of those great accidental discoveries? Was this how you made perfect, virgin grass, as Virgil thought you could make bees by beating the carcass of a lion to a pulp from which, as it decomposed, they would appear?

There was a bit on my lawn where a kind of coconut matting had started to grow, killing off the grass, so as an experiment I burnt it through, right down to the bare soil. It made a big patch, roughly the shape of Borneo. It is still there this year. Not only did the fine new grass which I now make effortlessly on the vegetable bed fail to appear: ordinary grass seed won't grow there either.

But the fact is I don't care about the lawn any more. We pioneers on the weed frontier have no time for such bourgeois concerns. I have to get this vegetable bed right. It's pretty good already. The only trouble is that actual vegetables spoil the look of the thing. The little neat rows that I have put in at one end—the usual things, lettuce, cabbage and stuff—not only interfere with my burning, they spoil the bare-soil look. They're green, too, same colour as the weeds.

I think I know what to do. I'll burn the whole lot once again, cabbages and all. Then I'll let that magical fine grass grow, and this can be my new lawn. Then I'll chomp up the old lawn with my machine, and I'll put the cabbages and things in there. *That'll* fox those damn weeds.

PANEGYRIC WORDS

¢ Thurber

I HAVE NO ambition whatsoever that one day on the front of 4 Prospect Place, a tall thin wooden house, like a cottage skyscraper, overlooking Hamsptead cemetery, there should be an LCC plaque saying anything but JAMES THURBER DINED HERE.

There is always a curious sense of anti-climax, of contraction, when one meets an admired writer, particularly one who creates a 'world' rather than just 'characters' (not that Thurber's grandfather, or Mrs Ulgine Barrows, or Walter Mitty, aren't characters. But people know what you mean when you say 'the Thurber world', as they do when you say 'the Kafka world', in fact come to think of it there are similarities). It still seems extraordinary to me that this elegantly grey-suited man, previously always first met in a hotel room where he was changing from one spotless white shirt into another, whom we now carefully guided (for he was blind) down our everyday stairs into our actual dining-room as he talked continuously in a kind of fast growl, was the single-handed creator of that extraordinary, so-familiar territory of bafflement somehow eased by laughter: the Thurber world.

His very name is one that, with his marvellous ear for the physical sound of words, he might have invented himself. It wouldn't be really surprising to learn that his real name was T. Smith or something, and that it was simply given to him to discover that what modern man does is to *thurb*. To thurb is to be soft and vulnerable, though not gormless or a professional 'little man', in a world of sharp objects, to be human among machines, to be peaceful among dangerous maniacs. It is to make indistinct sounds, T. S. Eliot's 'raids on the inarticulate'. It is to be simultaneously purposeful and bewildered. *Furry, burble, disturb, burthen, bother, brother, birth, throb, mother, father, curb, hither, thither, urban, trouble*—all these concepts are involved in the idea of thurbing. A thurber is one who, like the mass of men, lives a life 'of quiet desperation'. Who said that? I looked it up and it was on the same page in the *Penguin Dictionary of Quotations* as Thurber: H. D. Thoreau. The name Thoreau looks perfectly real, as do its companions James Thomson, 1700-1748 (*Rule, Britannia!*), James Thomson, 1834-1882 (*I find no hint throughout the universe/Of good or ill, of blessing or of curse/I find alone Necessity Supreme*), Rose H. Thorpe (*Curfew must not ring tonight*—and we all know who illustrated *that*; the thing is lousy with coincidence), Thucydides (*to famous men all the earth is a sepulchre*), Edward, First Baron Thurlow (*When I forget my sovereign, may God forget me*) and even the Rev. Godfrey Thring (*Fierce raged the tempest o'er the deep*). But the more one looks at the name *Thurber* on the page the less it seems like the name of a man and the more like some kind of function, attitude, atmosphere.

Thurber's world is such a compelling and recognizable one that, like all great artists, he makes one feel that it invented him instead of the other way round. Apart from anything else, Thurber stood for an Anglo-American consciousness and expressed it better than a hundred English-speaking Union manifestos. The Anglo-Saxons produced the world's first industrial civilization (if that is the word) utterly cut off from peasant roots. It's only now that France and Germany are going the same way (I keep reading sad articles about frozen chicken in once-famous *auberges*).

In the Columbus, Ohio, where Thurber grew up, fellow schoolboys 'could identify every car as it passed by: Thomas Flyer, Firestone-Colombus, Stevens Duryea, Rambler, Winton, White Steamer, etc.' Everything was already urban, ordinary, unmysterious, offering no place to the poet, the romantic, the inscrutable dreamer, 'and a wanderer who isn't inscrutable might just as well be back at Broad and High Streets in Columbus sitting in the Baltimore Dairy Lunch'. All previous civilizations have offered ordinary men some kind of inherited cosmology—heaven up there, hell down there, man in the image of God in the image of man, architecture with dear human squiggles, music as sung by imagined angels. But now universal cosmology is replaced by individual fantasies. And Walter Mitty can be claimed as the archetypal fantasist of this society.

He is a basic figure to set beside Faustus (archetypal intellect) or Don Juan (archetypal lust). People write whole plays and novels about him now (what is *Billy Liar* but Walter Mitty in three acts?). But for Thurber this was simply one perfect and elegant story (not much over two thousand words) in a torrent of equally acute (and blessedly funny) pieces.

Thurber also made us realize, quite painlessly, that the blue riband of sophisticated humour had crossed the Atlantic for the first time. The *ss Max Beerbohm*, a smart but elderly yacht full of upper-class dandies drinking sherry, but for years the fastest boat on the run, had suddenly been overhauled by this wonderful new liner, on which anyone with a sense of humour could travel free. Both ways. (Who has the riband now is open to doubt. There, as here, less and less wit finds its way into print, more and more into the better TV and radio scripts. If Thurber were a young man today the *New Yorker* wouldn't want to know him. 'It's mostly the childhood recollections of neurotic women now,' he said to me mournfully. And even Ross once called his drawings 'a fad of the English, a passing fancy'.)

He was a patriotic old American but I always felt he relished something, fast disappearing now, in the slowness of England, that traditional, backward-looking suspicion of gadgets, that refusal of dock-warehousemen to use fork-lift trucks instead of very old hand-trolleys, preferably with iron, tyreless wheels. The night he came to dinner (and it certainly *wasn't* an anti-climax) he talked a great deal about the longevity of English writers—not surprisingly, as he had been seeing Sir Compton Mackenzie; and he mentioned Eden Philpotts and Wodehouse.

'American writers of short pieces tend to drink Martinis as though the world were going to end tomorrow,' he said, 'and their idea of relaxation is *to wash a Venetian blind.*' A lot of this subsequently appeared in a piece in the *New Yorker*. Thurber's brain was restlessly at it all the time, making patterns against the great white vertiginous abyss of Nothing. When our docks get to accepting fork-lift trucks, any decade now, *we* shall have to face that Nothing too.

He told a wonderfully funny story about those hectic Jazz Age days, when he and his first wife went out to a restaurant with a friend who had recently married a Turkish girl. During the evening someone vomited over a balcony, unfortunately on to this girl. 'Her husband said, "You know, it's a terrible thing for a Moslem girl to be vomited on." My first wife said, "American girls aren't crazy about it, either."'

In *Babel: the Gate of the God*, by Gordon Bottomley (I am one of three living men who claim *The Waste Land* as the central poem of their experience and still like Georgian poetry, which wasn't *all* written by Sir John Squire) the giants are arguing:—

Then a lean giant 'Is not a calyx needful?'—
'Because round grapes on statues well expressed
Become the nadir of incense, nodal lamps,
Yet apes have hands that but and carved red crystals—
'Birds molten, touchly talc veins bronze buds crumble
Ablid ublai gham isz rad eighar ghaurl . . .'
Words said too often seemed such ancient sounds
That men forgot them or were lost in them;
The guttural glottis-chasms of language reached
A rhythm, a gasp, were curves of immortal thought.

Towards the end of his life, in blindness (with Helen Thurber always tactfully watching, ready to guide his hand to a glass, to warn about steps) he built (sometimes desperately) intricately interlocking battlements of words against chaos and Nothing. Words became *things* to him, and he built an extraordinary bridge between their thingness, their rightness, and the moral beauty of *order*. *The Wonderful O* seems to me a miraculous combination of moral fable, linguistic analysis, and of course laughter. As he wrote himself, 'the true balance of life and art, the saving of the human mind as well as of the theatre, lies in what has long been known as tragicomedy, for humour and pathos, tears and laughter are, in the highest expression of human character and achievement, inseparable'. The author of those luminous *Fables for Our Time,* the clear observer of sexual warfare, of muddled thought and non-communication, always longed for the sudden wonderful shout of laughter; he never got led into intellectual abstractions, because something remained eternally unspoiled in him. He always had this ambition to write the perfect piece about The Fight in The Grocery Store, even though he was aware that larger things than pyramids of cans may fall about our ears any day.

Let me end with the best Thurber moment I have ever known. It was one of my best theatre moments, too. *A Thurber Carnival,* for a variety of reasons, was a failure in this country. But I think of Betty Marsden reciting *The Last Flower*: perfectly straight, as Thurber's drawings were flashed on a screen. She came to the end:—

This time the destruction was so complete
That nothing at all was left in the world
Except one man
And one woman
And one flower

And there we sat, in front of that child's drawing of one bedraggled flower. There was total, intense silence for a moment, of the kind when your heart is everyone else's heart, you have got into another land. The thing so hoped for, so rare, in the theatre.

Not many people can do that *and* make you laugh. Thurber loved the human race; and it should love him back.

STENOGRAPHERS' WORDS

ℭ The Pseudo-Pitman

THE MOTHERS of many men now only middle-aged were once gentle stenographers, the first female entrants into commerce and industry. Did they co-operate blindly and passively when industry was replacing agriculture as the human norm, when the male, blacksmith's mystery of metal was forging a world in which art and feeling on the one hand, life and occupation on the other, became finally separated (for it is no good pretending there can be a great novel about a steelworks)? Did they leave no imperishable statement of gentle, ironic protest?

Indeed they did. In the midst of the mechanization of life, in the very act of co-operating with it (consciously or unconsciously) they wrote—hesitatingly at first, later with an extraordinary and gnomic precision—sentences of such classical randomness and clear idiosyncracy as to make a *haiku* appear woolly and self-indulgent. They captured their period for ever in a great poem. These are its opening stanzas:

1. *The rogue and the poor lame knave bear the cake to the door of the Room.*
2. *Joe Shaw bought the peach, the pear, the wreath, and the palm on the shore.*
3. *Otho should bathe in the pool, and Paul shear the sheep.*
4. *The Boer wrote an ode in a booth on the Vaal on 'A Tour in the Cape'.*
5. *Show the Jew the balm, the meal and the loaf.*

6. *In the cool of the day the boor and the fool rowed on the lake.*
7. *Esau should leave the Zoo and row on the Ouse.*
8. *A leech lay on the cheek of the pale female.*
9. *Joe and Jake hope to load the coke and coal in Poole in May.*
10. *The foal and the deer came to the shade of the oak on the road.*
11. *The heir showed the wreath to the page.*
12. *Job and Cato know the peak of the range.*
13. *The dame wore a veil, and bought a shawl on the pier.*
14. *Bear the bier of the peer to the coach.*
15. *The hero and the tall Zulu towed the boat in the teeth of the gale.*
16. *Show zeal, keep faith, and feel no shame.*

Up until now we have blindly regarded these lines as merely the opening exercise, on long vowels, in *Pitman's Shorthand Exercises.* Later ages (if there are any, if metal does not finally grind out human voices) will recognize them as the opening section of the masterpiece of the Pseudo-Pitman. Just as the Pseudo-Dionysius, whoever he may have been, is now accepted as an important voice of neo-Platonism, so the Pseudo-Pitman must inevitably emerge as a prime source for understanding the attitude of women (not the official, articulated 'feminist' position) at that fateful time when the factory, the metal world, was taking over.

The early stenographers (many are still living, grandmothers seen walking on to jet aircraft) are a mysterious link with the time before universal, both-sex employment. They came from families, one here, one there, in homes intensely local. Women's dresses faintly rustled, children laughed distantly in other rooms, figures with an extraordinary and definite life moved among mirrors on dark walls, in a light that seemed greenish after the brightness outside. That outside, that out-of-doors, was really no different from the outside where Reynolds posed his gentry with spaniels or Watteau his fragile picnickers. Some fathers worked, some did not; hardly any daughters did. We know surprisingly little about what everyone *did,* before everyone had a job, ultimately connected with metal.

This is the changing world preserved for ever by the Pseudo-Pitman's poem—or, more accurately, compilation; the printed text bears no attribution of authorship, and it is almost certainly the work of many hands, the corporate expression of these first stenographers. It is a classic expression of what Mumford calls the Neotechnic Age 'of the new economy, which began to emerge in the eighties, based on the use of electricity, the lighter metals, like aluminium and copper' (ah, yes, and the telephone, too; lighter metal filaments connecting our actual, invaded homes with the heavier clumps of the *first* metal takeover, of the Palaeotechnic Age of great thudding foundries, steelworks, gaunt railways).

It was no more conceived as 'art' than were those angels in the roof at Chartres which can be seen only by God. Nevertheless it is beyond dispute that masterly and anonymous editing has condensed into a poetic immediacy the ambivalence of these gentle, shirtwaisted stenographers at a watershed of Western, indeed world culture, embracing the universal modern (industrial) and the local ancient (agricultural) modes of life.

No single poet could have written like this. The style is both too general and too pure. It is an accretion, a distillation. Scores of years before Robbe-Grillet or

Burroughs there is (we are perhaps not surprised to find) a technique of alienation, a relentless elimination of the thread of personal narrative. The whole thing is very far removed from the manner of the old godlike, all-knowing novelists with whom it must be contemporary. The result is this cold, perfect evening pastoral.

We see that the old aristocratic order is passing. In a landscape recognizable for the last time as that of classical painting, where the foal and the deer come to the shade of the oak on the road, the old knightly customs are kept up, but only in a ghostly, funereal context. They bear the bier of the peer to the coach, and the heir shows the wreath to the page, but they are for the Arthurian shadows, and they know it, sadly. The upright old dowager, slightly mad, muttering to herself, wanders off to one of the growing popular 'seaside resorts' and, an incongruous figure among the tourists and day-trippers, vaguely buys a shawl on the pier. When the detritus of the funeral is washed up on the shore, perhaps of that very lake in which Excalibur was clutched by a hand clothed in white Samite, mystic, wonderful, the sturdy figure of Joe Shaw appears, coldly calculating its cost and souvenir value. He is sharply differentiated from those still living in the hieratic and settled class system based on land ownership; after the funeral the rogue and the poor lame knave bear the cake to the door of the Room, but they have an oddly superseded and archaic look, like the poor who appeared in England after the Dissolution of the Monasteries at the Reformation. Soon they too will migrate to the industrial cities.

Already the landscape has a depopulated and dreamlike air. Although the great house, with the Room facing the lake presenting blind and shuttered windows to the evening sun slanting over weed-grown terraces, is now the home only of birds and the occasional vagrant, and the boor and the fool are free to row on the lake where once laughing ladies with parasols were escorted over trim lawns to the elegant painted skiffs, a few sturdy yeomen, like Otho and Paul, carry on as if nothing had happened. Others, like Job and Cato, prepare resignedly for the countryman's changed status as an ornamental or holiday figure, a guide for city tourists vacationing in the mountains. Esau becomes frankly eccentric, loafing about, haunting zoos, his healthy rustic physique deteriorating for lack of exercise.

The newspaper and the telegraph are breaking down the old unique inviolacy of place. Instead of the historical, living time of one region we are in the instant, one-dimensional time of the world newsflash. Indeed, the Pseudo-Pitman in one single sentence gives an ironic summary of this, in a brilliant satire on every newsflash ever printed. For into the uneasy, doomed rural landscape there come rumours of global events too complex to be understood—hence the *superficial* newsflash. We are shown the Boer writing an ode on 'A Tour of the Cape' (this is the heyday of the 19th-century European empires, when vast static countries beckon to young active men in search of adventure and riches, crossing deserts, skirmishing with tribesmen, towing boats with tall Zulus in the teeth of gales; the final phase of Western expansion, before guilt and decline); but the shallow modern reader—or, more accurately, glancer—is not assumed to want to know who the Boer was, to learn what traditions have gone to the development of the Boer ode-form, to understand his culture, the background and the tensions capable (as we now know) of precipitating a full-scale war. The whole 'news interest' of this wickedly telling snippet is in the colourful, quirky, irrelevant detail that he wrote it in a booth on the Vaal.

We do not know *why* he wrote it in a booth; we do not even know his name. Yet so poignantly does the Pseudo-Pitman fix an era and its hidden regrets and attitudes, as mirrored in its subconscious, the minds of its 'disregarded' stenographers, that it is easy to overlook as merely a secondary literary virtue the incomparably sharp characterization (or, come to that, the marvellous aural music. Readers are recommended to read those sentences aloud). It may be an ironic newsflash, but it also gives an unforgettably clear picture of a bearded, slouch-hatted figure writing carefully in some kind of rude pavilion overlooking the Vaal river. We *know* him, he is instantly established, just like Otho, Paul, Job, Cato and the rest.

Yet for all 'his' almost contemptuous mastery of a supremely classical form, the Pseudo-Pitman is by no means unaware of contemporary Late Romantic theories. Just as Pater had written of the Mona Lisa 'set it for a moment beside one of those white Greek goddesses of beautiful women of antiquity, and how much they would be troubled by this beauty, into which the soul with all its maladies has passed! . . . she is older than the rocks on which she sits; like the vampire, she has been dead many times and learnt the secrets of the grave . . .' so also the Pseudo-Pitman is able subtly to shift the whole plane of this dazzling first page, to introduce a troubling and profound symbolism, making the, at first, clear and objective landscape seem to waver before our eyes and echo in our ears, with one deceptive and mysterious sentence; *show the Jew the balm, the meal, and the loaf*. Bottomless ambiguities of guilt and love!

This is one of two sentences in the imperative mood, artfully inserting a moral activism into the indicative scene-painting; and the more one looks at the other, concluding sentence, the more Sybilline it appears. On the face of it, *show zeal, keep faith, and feel no shame* is nothing but a Victorian pokerwork motto. Could it be, we then think, pure irony? Does the Pseudo-Pitman wish us to see the young stenographers as consciously and scornfully leaving their pre-industrial homes (*a leech lay on the cheek of the pale female* tells us as much about their stifling *ennui* as the entire career of a Dickens middle-class heroine)? We read the page again. No, surely there is no irony in the tender and nostalgic picture of the poor lame knave with which it opens.

In fact the Pseudo-Pitman recognizes the historical necessity of what is happening, and by these subtle imperatives, serious but not hectoring, a merely subjective regret for the old ways is avoided. All the same, the gentle but insistent human voice of the young stenographer is established firmly, on this very first page. The coming time of the complete dominance of metal, of the industrial city masses, is referred to only once, and then only in a harmless palaeotechnic—one might almost say pastoral context. Coke and coal, palaeotechnic symbols of the first Industrial Revolution, are lazily loaded by Joe and Jake in *Poole,* a small yachting harbour in the south of England, remote from the gaslit sweatshops and Bessemer furnaces of the industrial north (how many countries, symbolically, have an industrial north and a nostalgically pastoral south!). It is only later, as we shall see, that the impact of the inhuman, metallic mass-production future on a settled order is stated in more explicit rhythms. In this opening section it is not the new we see, but its shadow on the darkening landscape of the old.

O the young stenographers, O the memories still preserved in the hearts of those living grandmothers on the steps of jet aircraft! Memories given eternal form by their Pseudo-Pitman! Their middle-aged children, watching *their* children go *brrm brrm* with cars (and *a-a-a-a* with toy machine guns) know, perhaps with some regret, that there can be no more localization of consciousness, no more secret homes untouched by television. They do not need Marshall McLuhan, Vatican II or the Beatles (gorgeous, antique ceremonial chamberlains of the Order of the Holy British Empire, the first world-wide culture of steam and trousers) to tell them this (yet if only prayers to God in a thousand languages could somehow be routed through Telstar!).

When they started, these still living ex-stenographers were by no means the commonplace that stenographers (diluted as their craft is by little electronic machines) are today. They were within living memory of the *first* stenographers. Their elder colleagues, as one goes back in time, would have been ever rarer and rarer newcomers to industry from those secret homes. For already it had become necessary. They left these homes for offices which were across the way from factories of black and sometimes peculiarly red brick (some even had clock towers and ivy). A faint humming and thudding was perhaps all they heard from behind those walls. Or they would see, from their first-floor office windows, streams of men in cloth caps and overalls, walking or later on bicycles, at the hours, different from office hours, of factory shifts. Many of those moustachioed men perhaps would soon be photographed in khaki uniforms, serious or smiling outside tents. Motor cars, bicycles, typewriters and metal wars (shells for wartime, refrigerators for peace, as the sequence became) were being formed under those thwacking lines of overhead belting during the Neotechnic Age.

Local is slow and secret, international is instant and known to all.

It was inevitable. Various men since Archimedes had invented steam engines, and various men since Tiro, Cicero's secretary, had invented systems of shorthand; but when the time was ripe, in 1837, the steam engine (metal now mobile and organized) and shorthand came together, Isaac Pitman published his *Stenographic Soundhand*. Other systems were to follow; Sloan's adaptation of Duployé's method, the Sloan-Duployan, in 1882, Gregg's in 1888. There were the *Deutsche Kurzschrift* and many more. It is immaterial. In any case Pitman himself was not the author of our work; this can be proved on merely chronological evidence. He died in 1897 and could not, therefore, have written such a sentence as this, on the fourth page:

In the dispatch of Wednesday we read of air bombs on Smyrna.

The little pamphlet in which the Pseudo-Pitman's poem in its final, revised form appears bears on the cover the words 'Centenary Edition', although no date is given. Doubtless Pitman himself provided some of the raw material; or perhaps it might be more true to say that he bears the same relation to this mysteriously corporate work that Guido of Arezzo, the 11th-century monk doubtfully credited with the invention of the musical stave, bears to the great Western final flowering of the symphony. 1937, the centenary of Pitman's book, may well have been the date by which the metal age of universal, both-sex employment had reached its apogee—although the Smyrna sentence, for instance, obviously refers to the bloody siege of that city by the Turks in 1922, when 120,000 perished. By 1937 bombs had fallen, and were still to fall, on other cities besides Smyrna. This is a late interpolation; it is at the end of our period, not the beginning (the first 'modern' war, with its impersonal mechanical hail of metal, was, as Winston Churchill has pointed out, the American Civil War). We must not forget that the Pseudo-Pitman is concerned to show us the effect of the industrial age on the sensibilities of these virgin stenographers, not its final development. If we observe the whole page, with its cryptic title *Initial and Final Circles* (a reference both to Dante and to that cyclic fusion of the end with the beginning which obsessed men as different as Spengler and Eliot), we shall easily see that Smyrna (No. 13) and the other specifically 'metal' verse (No. 9) still occupy a marginal place.

1. *I love to listen to the sweet song sung by the skylark.*
2. *He has to take the boxes to the offices in Swain Avenue.*
3. *Our rugby team goes to Swansea on Tuesday and to Leeds on Saturday.*
4. *You can go with Joseph to the Rose Show on Saturday.*
5. *He insists on the dealer allowing the charges on the pipes and matches.*
6. *We can give a large bunch of roses to each of the boys.*
7. *You are likely to give annoyance to the fellow by talking in such a loud voice.*
8. *We hope to buy much of the rice and sago today.*

9. *The torpedoes, which the enemy use, are of a new design.*
10. *James hopes to show his canvas at the Academy.*
11. *You should sell the oils as soon as you can.*
12. *We can cash the six cheques at the bank in Cheapside tomorrow.*
13. *In the dispatch of Wednesday we read of air bombs on Smyrna.*
14. *The farm lad sold the pigs and the lambs at the fair.*
15. *We would like to emphasize the value of knowing all the rules in the book.*
16. *You are to go to Chiswick on Tuesday and to Keswick on Saturday.*
17. *Sam swam as far as the lock and back in an hour.*
18. *We can take the boxes of sauces to Swain and Roses on Monday.*

This page is also remarkable for the skill with which the *routine* of industrial life, in play as well as work, is depicted. Notice the references to Saturday in (3), (4) and (16), and the contrast between Sam's impulsive, old-time feat (17) of swimming to the lock and back and the contemporary organized sport such as the rugby football of (3). There is a delicate tension, too, between the farm life of (14) with its easy-going country flirtations (6) and the new suburban etiquette, in which the worst offence is to raise one's voice lustily, implicit in (7). We observe, too the detached irony of (15), the cynicism of 'playing it by the book' and the anti-climatic, dying fall of the last sentence (18), with its dreary sense of the ever-recurrent Monday, of inescapable routine dashing the hope of joyful freedom with which the passage so lyrically begins at (1).

Like any great work, the Pseudo-Pitman's poem may be opened anywhere; one may use it as the ancients used the *sortes vergilianae,* opening their Virgil at random and seeing significance in the first words that met their eyes. Yet there is, of course, a coherent thread. We do not arrive at the flat and somehow ominous calm of the passage just quoted with no transition from the opening pastoral. The young stenographers, pencils flying in the new tachygraphy produced by history to keep pace with the spinning overhead belting, might have looked out of their windows, from their offices with frosted glass partitions, brown linoleum, oak desks, tall typewriters with glass sides, candlestick telephones, in a slack moment, say at ten to four in the afternoon, a moment of *ennui,* and, aware of nothing but the humming and thudding of the factory across the road, they might have cried out in their hearts against routine, iron, the rule of metal. But their poet did not arrive at the protest against that boredom, with its Saturdays off, its dull trips to Chiswick,[1] its hopeless longing for the sweet song of the skylark, the wild country freedom canalized and deadened in the urban Rose Show, without an artistic bridge passage.

This is the second section, which describes the actual moment of the change.

1. *The fool full of punch and the poor fellow pull the bull into the pool.*
2. *Pack the lunch and get to the park.*
3. *Bang the door of the bank, and ring the bell in the rink.*
4. *Tom and Jim take the pony to the farm.*

[1] A suburb of West London.

5. *In dodging the shaggy dog the cook fell into the ditch.*
6. *Tommy Shipley and Jim Gill ring the bell, and bawl on the edge of the meadow.*
7. *The picnic in the woody dell became a monthly affair.*
8. *Mary took the lunch to the far meadow.*
9. *Eric and Dora dwell on the muddy bank of the Cam.*
10. *The leafy cabbage, the ruddy berry, and bunch of weed belong to the lazy farm lad.*
11. *Judge Jerry and the jury were weary of the wary cabby, and readily took leave of the worry and monotony.*
12. *The village worthy brought the tall fir into the wood.*
13. *The coach and four, and the car carry the poor to York in the month of March.*
14. *The monkey, the buffalo, the gorilla, and the kangaroo were in the zoo.*
15. *The King and the Admiral love to live in the ship.*
16. *Fanny read many a big book to cull a theme on melody.*
17. *A cuckoo and a lark perch on the top of the bush.*
18. *The fish Ted bought were cod, haddock, hake, roach and herring.*
19. *Bewail the death of the notary and show pity, love, mercy and charity.*
20. *Annie and Minnie know the date of the party.*

Violence and hysteria mark the change from the old order. Nothing is safe or secure any more. Even though the picnic in the woody dell becomes a monthly affair, it is disturbed by gangs of drunken louts, threatening the prim excursionists with their packed lunches by bawling and ringing bells on the edge of the meadow, causing at least one nervous member of the party, Mary, to get as far away from them as possible (8). Authority seems powerless to deal with them (even servants are no longer to be trusted, but fall drunkenly into ditches); they range the unsettled countryside unchecked, banging on the doors of banks and ringing bells in rinks. It is not likely that such men will be mollified by patronizingly cheap trips arranged for the poor in ramshackle transport, to places like York in the off-peak season (13). Those who are not uprooted seek solace, like Annie and Minnie, in a hectic round of parties and picnics (20). For every yeoman true to the old ways, like Tom and Jim, there are a dozen disaffected farm lads, letting weeds grow among the cabbages, joining the urban gangs, crazed with punch, firing hayricks and drowning valuable livestock.

The administration breaks down. Political bosses like the notorious (we may assume) 'Judge' Jerry make a mockery of the old careful processes of law, impatient as they are to get off to some orgy themselves (11). It is useless to bewail the death of the notary (and probably dangerous when Judge Jerry's men are around; better ask no questions). The old ruling classes have abdicated; the King and the Admiral (15), decadent gigglers at the end of a lusty line, wait on their yacht for the news of the march on the palace, the end of the old order.

Later this unrest is described in literal, almost prosaic terms:

Unrest grows stronger and stronger; sobriety and wisdom take wings and fly; the screech and scream of the leaders cause the miner to overlook his duty to his master, and his distressed family. Wiseacres display a noticeable distrust of any measures for lessening the cause of strikes; but some day, however, we hope all differences among masters and miners may be less possible, and discriminate measures passed by our supreme authority, which will for ever dispel the inevitable sorrows of a prolonged and bitter struggle.

We are dealing, of course, with a period before socialism had emerged as an articulate and powerful, not to say respectable creed.

This later, editorializing style is very well integrated with the aphoristic beginning. The earlier style recurs continually. The next section but one depicts, in six marvellous opening sentences, the violence now absorbed, as newspaper-reported crime in a newspaper-reading, world-and-trade-conscious urban culture.

1. *The pun of the puny fellow revives the jokes of John Brown who lives in Sydney Avenue, Croydon.*[2]
2. *The Czar's wife is known as the Czarina, and the wife of the Sultan as the Sultana.*
3. *The villainy of the villain mystifies the policeman of Stepney.*[3]
4. *In the form of foreign produce we receive grain, semolina, coffee, wine, mutton and beef.*
5. *Others take from us, in return, linen and cotton fabrics, iron and tin wares.*

The editorializing style, once established, enables the Pseudo-Pitman to introduce episodic or biographical strophes, like that concerning Isaac Bassett, a scientist:

Isaac Bassett resides on the right bank of the

[2] A suburb of south London.
[3] A borough of metropolitan London.

Mersey. He is a modest scientist, and we fear his modesty is a loss to science.

Bassett is the old type of natural philosopher:

He perused many essays on botany, and purposed issuing a volume on the animals of Assam and Siam.

But such a gentle figure is out of place in the world that is now emerging:

The onsets of his enemies became so numerous and so libellous, he eventually evinced no desire to bestow his time on the topic.

Fortunately he has private means;

He was in receipt of an annual income: the legacy of a solicitor of Sussex.

Isaac Bassett is altogether a more sympathetic figure than that, alas more typical of the period, of the self-made Henry Hobbs:

The life of Henry Hobbs shows how a hapless lad may by means of grit, rise from poverty to riches. He was the son of a huckster, and he belonged to a family who had no aspiration to make any headway in life. His home was a mere hovel.

But he prospers, doubtless because of a certain strain of ruthlessness.

On finishing his training he was successful in obtaining a post at Halifax. Here he showed ample ability, and his employer, Hardy Higgins, placed him at the head of his factory. This caused a hub-

bub among the men, but Henry was able to live it down.
His tastes are varied, but music is his chief hobby. Now he owns a factory, and his home is 'The Hall' on the hill at Harley Heath, in the neighbourhood of Holbeck.

The Pseudo-Pitman does not actually say that Hobbs bought out Hardy Higgins, nor is there any but the subtlest of indications that music may have been much the most respectable of his 'varied tastes'; but somehow we are left in no doubt that this is an altogether less desirable character than Isaac Bassett, who used his Sussex solicitor's legacy thus:

Some of the sum, we assume, he used to satisfy life's necessities; the residue sufficed to endow a dwelling at the seaside in Essex, to house invalid analysts. Many a storm-tossed hero cherishes his purity, meekness and kindness.

However, this is not a poem of despair. The Pseudo-Pitman, for all the acute observation of the pastoral world that industry is destroying, never relinquishes an underlying note of acceptance, a gentle female determination to humanize the new environment. Somehow whatever happens, the young stenographers, experienced in but not brutalized by it, come to terms; for they are forever poised to desert from it, to become mothers of families still possessing something of that secret, unknown quality of the ones in which *they* were young, when it was all beginning. Perhaps nothing is more moving than the moment where the rarely voiced 'I' of the poem makes the only actual reference to love in the whole work, the shy avowal which appears with such sudden and astonishing effect at the very end (No. 10) of the following section:

1. *The Brothers Oliver belong to a clever family. They live close to Frome*[4], *and they treasure the visits paid to Ilfracombe*[5], *as bright flashes in a life of increasing labour and decreasing leisure.*
2. *On Friday last they sailed on the Bristol Channel and passed many vessels lying safely at anchor.*
3. *Among the trippers on the boat was a labour leader, an omnivorous newspaper reader. He looked gravely at the elder Oliver as he said he disliked to see brutal criminal cases so eagerly read by divers classes of society.*
4. *At three o'clock dinner he discussed the deplorable growth of gambling, ascribing it, in a minor degree, to the evil effects of the Press.*
5. *This was a trifle vexing to a fellow visitor, residing in the cathedral city of Gloucester, so he raised his voice in favour of the Press, and said he was bitterly opposed to such attacks, as they were utterly unpardonable and were simply carried on to satisfy a desire to announce a clique of persons eager to frame a propaganda to solve the pressing problems of the labouring classes of society.*
6. *A cavil followed, causing the loss of valuable time, and producing mirth among the persons at the table.*
7. *To stop this ridiculous reasoning Fred Oliver addressed the gathering. He himself was no orator, he said, and he was afraid he lacked the ability to take up the cudgels on either side.*

[4] A west-country town.
[5] A west country watering place.

8. *He spoke of the regrettable feeling the speakers brought to bear on the topic, and said patience was of admirable service in a gathering of thinkers and discussers of opposite views.*
9. *This seasonable advice was unassailable, and the excessive zeal of the rivals was suitably denounced in able speeches by Frank Oliver and Michael Fleming.*
10. *Michael is principal of a large firm and I myself think much of him.*

(This section is slyly titled *Initial Hooks: Alternative Forms.*)

Many gentle stenographers did not pass their whole lives among bales, overhead belting and old oak desks.

Messrs Brant and Prout are large dealers in hats.

The fool drank pale ale at the end of a hard day, and crashed his car into the bar.

Your grandfather and I speak often of the small bright clouds above the bay, on a certain day at Ilfracombe.

Place six dozen cases of ketchup in the wire basket and call for the check, Will.

Let us praise the piety and calm of good mothers.

Michael proposed to me in the corridor beyond the loading bay.

It is now possible to transmit speech at a speed unassimilable by the human ear.

The lad in the jet is Sam, my second grandson.

Let us gaze into the sky above the farm and hear the sound of the lark.

Some silos are stocked with cereals; others, we may assume, secrete swift military missiles.

The ancient Chinese, believing that metal was a concentration of the earth's life, used to place a human embryo in a new furnace in order to restore that which they had taken.

On a fine Saturday I wore a gay hat and met Michael at the Rose Show.